God's Impatience in Liberia

Church Growth Series

Church Growth in Mexico: Donald McGavran, John Huegel,
   Jack Taylor

Wildfire—Church Growth in Korea: Roy E. Shearer

New Patterns of Church Growth in Brazil: William R. Read

Church Growth in Central and Southern Nigeria: John B. Grimley, Gordon E. Robinson

God's Impatience in Liberia: Joseph Conrad Wold

God's Impatience
in Liberia

by

JOSEPH CONRAD WOLD

1368

WILLIAM B. EERDMANS PUBLISHING COMPANY
GRAND RAPIDS, MICHIGAN

FOREWORD

Here is a book to be read and pondered by all interested in the Christian mission. It closely intertwines mission fact and mission theory: what has happened and what should happen. The book speaks to a major missionary problem: In a land favorable to the Christian religion, where mission work has been carried on for many years, and national Churches have long been in charge, how is it possible for the Christian religion to stop precisely among those who are most Christianized? When the leadership becomes Christian in large measure, why has the Christian religion not spread to the remaining nine-tenths of the people? What stops it now? What are the ways in which it will spread— if it spreads? And the other ways which effectively block the communication of the Gospel, even while many are working and praying toward that end?

These pertinent questions face missions everywhere in the world. Pastor Wold's book is an accurate, reliable description of the spread of the Church in Liberia; but the issues it illumines are not confined to that land. They confront mission (and, unresolved, impede and arrest mission) in most countries of the earth. Mission executives, missiologists, missionaries, and ministers of both younger and older Churches everywhere should read *God's Impatience in Liberia,* for He is impatient in other places also.

Thirty years ago, the great Bishop Azariah wrote, "God alone can touch the hearts of people. The forces that make for change of religious allegiance on the part of men are many and often beyond human analysis. [Yet there are] lines along which Christ's followers may intelligently cooperate with Him in accomplishing His purposes for mankind. It is our duty to watch the movements of the Spirit, lest we frustrate God's work by our unbelief, indifference, or mismanagement of potential situations."

5

3 1852

Anyone who reads Mr. Wold's book will come to have a new understanding of the lines along which Christ's followers may cooperate intelligently with Him in accomplishing His urgent purposes in every land.

—DONALD MCGAVRAN, Dean
School of World Mission
and Institute of Church Growth
Fuller Theological Seminary
Pasadena, California

CONTENTS

INTRODUCTION

In one of the parables of the New Testament the "Kingdom of God" is compared to a mustard seed "which, when it is sown in the earth, is less than all of the seeds of the earth: but when it is sown, it groweth up and becometh greater than all herbs." It is also said that: "The Kingdom of God . . . is like leaven, which a woman took and hid in three measures of meal, till the whole was leavened. . . ." Christianity began as a small Jewish sect, looked at askance by the leaders of the nation, numerically the least considerable of the many faiths and religious societies of the recently founded Roman Empire. Yet, geographically, it has spread more widely than any other religion in all the millenniums of mankind's long history.*

In our century, which has seen the rise and spread of communism, the emergence of numerous newly independent nations, and the invention not only of radio, the airplane, miracle drugs, and other such wonders, but even the harnessing of the inner forces of the atom, we are apt to forget that one of the truly amazing phenomena of the twentieth century is the continuing spread of Christianity around the world. This spread of the Christian faith, and accompanying expansion of the Church, has been part and parcel of the very nature of Christianity from the day of Pentecost. But in the modern missionary movement it has reached new, undreamed-of proportions.

Perhaps because it is so big, the present-day missionary endeavor the world over is sometimes in danger of losing sight of the leaven-in-the-dough nature of the Christian faith. The evangelistic purpose and goal of the Church is obscured at times

* Kenneth Scott Latourette, *A History of the Expansion of Christianity*, Vol. 1, *The First Five Centuries* (New York: Harper & Brothers, 1937), p. ix.

by the "good missionary work" that needs doing; and the growth of the Church slows down while leaders work out administrative machinery for the younger Churches to take over.

Slow growth is a serious but curable disease. Its needless continuance surely tests God's patience. The roll of writers who have protested against this trend and diagnosed its causes includes nearly every major mission theorist and most minor ones. A smaller number of men have described and advocated cures. One such cure is the rapid "spontaneous" expansion of the Church in non-Christian lands by people movements. Roland Allen, J. Waskom Pickett, and Donald A. McGavran are among the notable advocates of this approach. Dr. McGavran in particular has clarified the "church growth point of view," which is that the expansion of the Church (in terms of actual numbers of persons baptized, attending church, and taking communion; of congregations established, churches built, and pastors trained) is one valid criterion by which to appraise the faithfulness of the Church in any given land. Proponents of this view do not claim that it is the only criterion of the Church's faithfulness, but that it must be taken into account. This sharp, rule-of-thumb type of measurement and approach toward church expansion is not the daily bread of church life but a tonic for the sickness of stunted growth.

The point of view presented in the following pages is an analysis and preliminary prescription for slow growth among the Churches in the African country of Liberia, the oldest independent native democracy on that continent, with many ties to the United States. My contention is that

1. Church growth has not taken place in Liberia to the extent that might have been expected, or in proportion to the existing potential in past years.

2. In Liberia today church growth is both possible and probable; indeed, it appears that God Himself urgently, yes, impatiently desires it.

3. The Churches in Liberia can and should take steps to realize growth commensurate with the opportunities the situation affords.

Every population is different. The Church does not grow in

the same way or at the same rate in any two places in the world, or at any two different times in history. By examining the situation and the rate and pattern of church growth that has taken place in it, one may determine whether or not the Church has been faithful to its missionary calling. In some populations, circumstances make expansion all but impossible, and the church growth researcher can conclude that explanations are not merely excuses; the Church has been faithful, yet for good reason there has been slow growth. In populations which show clear signs of being open to the Gospel, however, when the Church expands slowly the criterion of growth may expose weak explanations and mere excuses. When, in the mysterious providence of God, the fullness of time has come, then churches should multiply.

This book is one of the Church Growth Series, each of which describes accurately the genesis and development of the Church or Churches in some land and thus extends understanding of the task of mission in them. In the bibliography, under the heading "Mission Theory—Church Growth," books of this series are marked by two asterisks. More church growth researches are under way. A body of tested knowledge, concerning the ways and patterns which God is blessing to the spread of the Church, is rapidly coming into existence.

I tender this understanding of Christian mission to my fellow Christians—nationals and missionaries—in the hope that they will see in it an attempt to forward the King's business, and may find light not only for the Christianization of the tribes in Liberia, but also perhaps for that vast enterprise into which God directs His Church: world mission.

I must take this opportunity to acknowledge my indebtedness to those without whose help this book would never have been written. From the first day I received his letter advising me of the Institute of Church Growth and the possibility of a Liberian church growth research fellowship, Dr. Donald A. McGavran has been a constant source of inspiration. For the research fellowship I wish to thank both Northwest Christian College, which originally gave the grant and provided the facilities for carrying out the research, and the School of World Mission at Fuller Theological Seminary, which upon the transfer of the

Institute of Church Growth to its Pasadena campus is publishing the book in the Church Growth Series. I am especially
grateful to the Board of World Missions of the Lutheran
Church in America for granting this furlough study year and
paying all the necessary travel expenses.

—J. C. WOLD

Zorzor, Liberia

CHAPTER I

THE LAND AND ITS HISTORY

If any country in the world can be said to be open to the Gospel, Liberia is that country. The government has formulated wise policies which encourage missions and missionaries. These are matched by an open, friendly acceptance of missionaries on the part of the people themselves. Goods for mission and church work can be brought into the country duty-free. Officials, from the Secretary of Education on down to the immigration officer and the village chief, will all go out of their way to assist a missionary. Liberians recognize the missionary as a friend.

Any American will be impressed by the tremendous reservoir of good will Liberians have toward the United States. This close relationship has arisen naturally and can be explained historically by the fact that most of the original colonists were free Negroes from America, and by the more important fact that since Liberian independence in 1847 the relationship has been that of independent nations. In spite of great discrepancies of wealth and size, this relation has been one of mutual respect. The good will may also be attributed to the fact that the first and in many cases the only white men Liberians have known were missionaries and not colonial government officials.

Liberians themselves have little race prejudice. Moreover, in spite of the suspicion raised by news reports of bad race relations in the United States, prejudice is not something a Liberian expects or experiences from whites. The lack of tension has a beneficial effect on all parties, including the white missionary.

President William V. S. Tubman is an active Methodist lay preacher. Vice President W. R. Tolbert is president of the World Baptist Alliance, and nearly all the leaders of the country are church members. Liberians consider their country a Christian nation. Religious instruction is required in the public schools. Missions and Churches are encouraged to operate institutions supported partly—in a few cases entirely—by government funds. In times like these, when countries around the world are limiting the number of missionaries who may enter their borders, and when "Yankee, go home!" is a popular slogan, Liberia stands out for its friendly attitude toward Americans and most especially toward missionaries.

Thus the situation has definite implications for mission boards and Churches with work in Liberia. While they must never presume upon the friendship, it is to be earnestly hoped that they will rise to take advantage of the opportunities it affords, for surely the Church should grow well and flourish in such a favorable environment.

The total membership of the Churches in Liberia is high compared with some of its neighbors. (Guinea: 16,843 Protestants and 25,100 Roman Catholics, or 1.3 per cent of a total estimated population of approximately 3 million. Ivory Coast: 83,918 Protestants and 298,734 Roman Catholics, or 13 per cent of a total estimated population of 3 million. Sierra Leone: 61,111 Protestants and 18,545 Roman Catholics, or 3.2 per cent of a total population of 2,450,000. Liberia, with 114,049 Protestants and 12,804 Roman Catholics, has 12.6 per cent of a total population of about 1 million.[1]) However, expansion of the Churches has been limited almost entirely to the Americo-Liberians or "the civilized element" near the coast. Liberian church membership includes only a small per cent of the tribal people of the hinterland.

To what may we attribute this slow, socially stratified growth of the Church? Can anything be done to change the pattern of growth that has characterized the Churches in this country? The Church must seek explanations from the past that will guide it to the formulation of new and vital policies for making disciples in Liberia.

For a new day has dawned. The factors that inhibited the growth of the Churches are lessening, in some cases disappearing entirely. Those that encourage church growth remain and are becoming more influential. My studies lead me to believe

---

[1] Kenneth Grubb, ed., *World Christian Handbook, 1962* (London: World Dominion Press, 1962).

that Liberia is on the brink of a tremendous turning to Christ. Whole villages, even whole clans, are ready to renounce ancestor spirit worship and turn to Christianity. I am further convinced that this kind of rapid church growth is not only possible but desirable here—God desires it. Indeed, God is impatient to see His tribesmen march into His Church. They are His lost children.

The Churches, which in the future will be led more by Liberians than by foreign missionaries, must see the opportunities and grasp them. They must disciple all the tribes, until one nation, united in Him who is the only source of real unity, moves unafraid to claim the promises of tomorrow.

Let us then proceed to look more closely at the land and the people, as a first step in understanding the patterns which will deter or augment church growth. The Church always grows in specific populations each with characteristics and circumstances that distinguish it from all other populations. Each population has its own ways of responding to or resisting the Gospel. To understand the particular problems of church growth in Liberia, we must look at the environment in which the Church must grow. The land, the people, and the Churches and missions themselves, all are factors to consider before proposing a plan for church growth.

THE LAND

In many ways Liberia is unique among African nations, yet it is very much a part of the continent. It is a small country—43,000 square miles, about the size of the state of Ohio; only four other African states have a smaller territory. The population is approximately one million.

However, Liberia has an influence on African affairs and indeed on world affairs out of all proportion to its size. In an Africa of newly independent nations, thirty-four since 1951, Liberia was the first, and for more than a hundred years the only independent African state. It shares many of the problems of development that plague other emerging nations: high illiteracy rate; high infant mortality (50 per cent in the first two years of life); low per capita income ($140 in 1961); low production, with too great a dependence upon a few raw materials; and shortage of skilled personnel. In seeking solutions to these problems, Liberia is handicapped neither by violent anticolonialism nor by the naive utopias that obsess some of her newly independent neighbors.

The earliest Portuguese explorers described and drew pictures of prominent features along the Liberian coast as they made their way down around the bulge of West Africa. They called it the "grain coast" because of a grain-sized spice that was traded there. However, any advantages that may have accrued from those early trade relations paled into insignificance in the horrors of the nearly two centuries of slave trade that followed. One classic account of that trade, *The Journal of a Slave Trader* by Newton, is the log of a slave ship written while it lay at anchor near St. John's River, Cape Palmas, Mesurado Cape, St. Paul River, River Cestos, and so on, all in Liberia.[2] The trade in human beings and accompanying tribal wars devastated the population. Liberia remains underpopulated even today.

The country is located low down to the west on the bulge of Africa, its coastline running northwest to southeast, to the point where the edge of the continent finally turns eastward for more than a thousand miles. Liberia faces out to the Atlantic toward the corresponding bulge of South America. It has about 350 miles of coast and extends inland to a depth of between 100 and 150 miles. Lying between 4°22' and 8°33' north of the equator, the climate is tropical. The mean temperature is 82°F., and along the coast there is an almost constant sea breeze. The annual rainful exceeds 180 inches at the coast, but places in the interior receive as little as 70 inches. There are two seasons. During the rainy season, between the months of April and October, it rains nearly every day. In the dry season, from November to March, the dust-laden wind from the Sahara, called the Hamartan, sometimes blows, and relative humidity may drop to as low as 30 per cent.[3]

[2] John Newton, *The Journal of a Slave Trader (1750-1754)*, Bernard Martin, ed. (London: Epworth Press, 1962).

[3] Louis Barron, ed., *Worldmark Encyclopedia of the Nations—Africa* (New York: Harper & Row, 1963), pp. 124-27.

Along the length of the coast lies a belt of mangrove marshes, shallow lagoons, and tidal creeks about thirty miles wide. Behind this the land rises steeply to a zone of undulating tropical forest that ranges in elevation from six hundred to a thousand feet. Further inland the land rises again to a plateau of fifteen hundred to two thousand feet above sea level. On the Guinea border, the Nimba range rises again to 4,200 feet. Six major rivers flow across the country at right angles to the coastline. Only the Cavala, which forms the boundary between Liberia and Ivory Coast, is navigable, and that only for a few miles.[4]

Trees grow well in Liberia. Africa's greatest high forest stretches across the country and her neighbors. Timber is one of her most valuable undeveloped resources, and tree crops provide nearly half the total exports. The leading forest product is, of course, rubber, grown on several hundred private rubber farms as well as a number of large commercial plantations, of which Firestone's, with a 200,000-acre tract under cultivation, is the largest in the world. Rubber production is still expanding, and in 1965 the first trees on the Goodrich plantation began producing latex. There are large coffee and cocoa plantations throughout the country. The sweet fragrance of coffee blossoms fills the air even on forest paths in the interior; and cocoa, spread on mats to dry in the sun, is a common sight in the streets of any village. The red oil and palm butter made from the meat on the outside of the palm nut are used almost exclusively in village cooking. The inner palm kernel, with the shell cracked off, is another important export.

The verdant luxury of the forest belies the unproductive laterite earth that lies beneath the surface. Cleared of forest and exposed to sun, air, and rain, the nutrients are soon leached from the soil, which bakes hard as brick. Cleared land will produce a crop of upland rice only the first year. After that it must be allowed to grow back to forest for at least seven years before it can be farmed again. However, government experiment stations throughout the country, and teams of Nationalist Chinese farmers, have demonstrated that paddy rice farming can produce

[4] *Ibid.*, p. 126.

abundant crops over and over on the same land. This method
may alleviate the problem of low agricultural production.

The forests are alive with more than two hundred species of
birds and a large variety of jungle animals. Since the villagers
depend on wild game to supplement their diet, large animals are
scarce near the settlements, where men seldom walk any distance without a shotgun slung across their shoulders. Leopards
still roam deep in the forest, and two men who had been gored
by elephants were treated at the Lutheran hospital in Zorzor
during 1964. Monkeys are common pets and may be seen on
the porches of village houses, or even clinging to the top of a
public bus as it drives along the road. A baby chimpanzee can
be yours for twenty-five dollars. The pygmy hippopotamus, native only to Liberia, and several dozen other species of animals
are exhibited in the President's private zoo at Totota. The royal
antelope, hero of many African folk stories, lives in the forest.
It is the smallest member of the deer family, the adult male
measuring only ten inches high at the shoulder. Fish are abundant in the rivers and streams, and the waters off the coast teem
with fish, but this is another resource not yet developed com-
mercially. Termite hills eight and ten feet high are common in
the forests. Columns of driver ants are likely to be encountered
on any forest path. The tsetse fly occurs along certain river
banks, and mosquitoes, including the malaria mosquito, are also
present in the country.

EARLY HISTORY

The story of the modern state of Liberia and its beginnings
may be traced back to America and the antislavery movement
there. Slavery had outspoken opponents in America from the
time it was first introduced. Many slaveholders left wills freeing
their slaves as a kind of final act to satisfy their uneasy consciences. George Washington himself left such a will. The idea
of a colony in Africa where free Negroes could settle was set
forth by some preachers even before the Revolutionary War.

By 1808, Americans were forbidden to participate in the
slave trade, and the open importation of African slaves ceased.
Freedom is the enemy of slavery. The presence of free Negroes

in a society where others were still held in bondage was embarrassing to some and a threat to the property of others. Thomas Jefferson was one of many who were convinced that the best solution was to assist freed Negroes to return to Africa. In 1817 the American Colonization Society was formed and $100,000 appropriated by the Congress to establish such a colony. Not all those who pressed for its establishment were motivated by sympathy and philanthropy. There had been bloody slave uprisings in Virginia, and among those who contributed most toward the Colonization Society were owners who had the most to lose from a slave revolt.[5]

Not all former slaves or their children wanted to go back to Africa. There were some who chose to stay and claim a share of the rewards in the rich new nation their labor had contributed so much to develop. But others felt that their only hope of real liberty lay in returning to the continent of their origin. Promoters of the colony often painted an overbright picture of what life there would be like. Thus, with a hope born of idealism and despair, in 1820 the first intrepid band of settlers crossed the Atlantic. They first stopped near Freetown, Sierra Leone, where the British had already established a similar colony, but were refused settling rights there. They sailed on down the coast. Twenty-two of the Negroes and all the whites who accompanied them died before they finally found a chief who was willing to sell them the right to settle. The survivors bought a strip of land 140 miles long by 40 miles wide for an assortment of goods worth about three hundred dollars.

They settled on Providence Island at the south of the Mesurado River. Here they founded what is today the capital city, Monrovia, named after the fifth president of the United States. They called their country Liberia from the word liberty. The country's founding fathers had a Zionist-like understanding of their divine destiny in establishing the colony. They felt themselves called to carry Christianity to Africa, and to abolish slavery at its source. This missionary zeal sustained them in

[5] Walter Cason, "The Growth of the Church in the Liberian Environment" (unpublished Ph.D. thesis, Columbia University, 1962), Chap. II, pp. 10-42.

their encounters with what must have seemed insuperable obstacles.

The national motto of Liberia is: "The love of liberty brought us here," and the nation's history proves that this is no empty phrase, for men must love freedom a great deal to suffer for it as those first colonists suffered. Though the coast of West Africa was called "the white man's grave," skin color had nothing to do with it. It was the grave of Negroes, too. The colonists literally faced death to seek liberty on those hostile shores. Between 1820 and 1840, 4,456 Negroes were sent to Liberia by the colonization societies; 2,198, or nearly half, died.[6] Malaria, two kinds of dysentery, and yellow fever were the chief killers. There were no doctors. There were no stores from which to buy clothes, tools, or weapons. The crops they raised were scarcely enough to feed them and left little or nothing for barter with the ships that stopped to trade and bring more colonists. What little was sent by the philanthropic societies was barely enough to give the newcomers a start.

From the first the indigenous tribes were hostile and made frequent raids. They vastly outnumbered the colonists. Indeed, if they had not been at war with one another and had united against the colony, it is doubtful whether it could have survived. During one raid, when its very existence seemed threatened, Matilda Newport saved the day by putting a torch to a cannon and firing into the attacking horde. She became a national heroine, and Matilda Newport Day is a Liberian holiday celebrated on December first each year. Her deed is only one of hundreds but has come to symbolize the determination and courage that founded the nation. The hostility between the settlers and the tribal people sowed the seeds of fear and suspicion, vestiges of which remain even today, and constitute a disruptive influence. This tension has surely been one of the factors that explain the slow development of the Churches among the tribes of Liberia.

In 1847, twenty-seven years after the first settlers arrived, the

[6] Harold Vink Whetstone, *Lutheran Mission in Liberia* (Philadelphia: Board of Foreign Missions of the United Lutheran Church in America, 1955), p. 47.

country declared its independence under a constitution patterned after that of the United States. Although Britain and France were among the first countries to recognize the new nation, they did not really take seriously the idea of an independent Negro state on a continent of colonies. Had Liberia retained a colonial tie with the United States, France and Britain would have had the United States to reckon with in disputes over boundaries and import duties; but in dealing with a tiny defenseless country, they could use any excuse to seize large sections of territory and interfere in its internal affairs without fear of retribution.

The moral responsibility some American statesmen felt toward Liberia was diluted by the fact that it was thousands of miles away; and indeed, some Americans, for various reasons, would have rejoiced to see the experiment fail. When, in the case of territorial encroachment by European powers, America did make diplomatic objections, they were too timid and too late to be effective. Diplomacy, however, did much to preserve the country's autonomy. Liberia had able leaders. President J. J. Roberts won the respect of the colonial powers with his eloquent defense of his nation's rights. But he had no gunboats to back up his words. The rivalry between the British and the French led one to object whenever the other came too close to swallowing the whole cake. Only the fact that her enemies were divided kept the country from disappearing altogether.

Until 1908, Liberia did not even have an army to keep internal order. In that year the Frontier Force was organized, with a British officer in command and men who had served with Sierra Leone forces in the ranks. The French objected to this obvious attempt at a British take-over. They demanded, and obtained, a position for a French officer in the force. About this time Germany was carving out an empire for herself in Africa and had her own designs on the precariously situated little republic, up to the outbreak of World War I.

Liberia declared war on Germany shortly after the United States, and Liberian troops saw action in France. Monrovia was actually shelled by a German submarine. After the war, Liberia became a member of the League of Nations. It remained neutral through most of World War II, but cooperated actively enough with the United States to prompt the Germans to make radio broadcasts to its citizens urging them to revolt.

President Roosevelt visited Liberia in 1943, and President Barclay of Liberia returned the visit later that same year. He was accompanied by the then President-elect, William V. S. Tubman. Liberia was one of the Allies, having declared war on Germany in January of 1944, and so became a charter member of the United Nations when it was formed. Since then it has played an increasingly active role in world affairs.[7]

The year 1944 was auspicious for Liberia. World War II was ending; construction of the Freeport harbor at Monrovia was begun with Lend-Lease funds, and President Tubman took office. Since then, only one word describes what has happened to this vigorous African country: change. Social, economic, and cultural changes have been taking place at an unbelievably rapid pace. They are so far-reaching that serious descriptions of Liberia as recent as that written by Raymond L. Buell in 1947 are so outdated as to sound like a ludicrous parody to anyone who has lived there only since 1960.[8] No visitor to Monrovia can help but be impressed by the number of large, beautiful new buildings. Not only the magnificent President's mansion and government buildings, but new storefronts and private housing alike give the impression that this country is "going places."

There is change in more than Monrovia's skyline. Even in the far interior there are new schools in the villages along recently opened roads. Mission pilots who fly near the northern border say they can tell when they have accidentally strayed across onto the Guinea side of the border by looking down on a village. If there are only thatched houses they turn back. Liberian villages have many corrugated iron roofs.

In 1947 Buell wrote that Liberia had no roads, no hotels, no medical profession, no teacher's college . . . no census, no roads

---

[7] Lawrence A. Marinelli, *The New Liberia* (New York: Frederick A. Praeger, 1964), Chap. IV, pp. 100ff.

[8] Raymond Leslie Buell, *Liberia: A Century of Survival, 1847-1947* (Philadelphia: University of Pennsylvania Press, 1947).

in the interior, no railroad, few able men at the top, and not even a diplomatic mission in Washington.[9] A list of the accomplishments of the Tubman administration reads like an itemized answer to this criticism, with many additions. What has been done would be an achievement in any country, but in the light of Liberia's previous situation and history it is nothing short of amazing.

What hindered its earlier development? From the first, the new venture in Liberia was crippled by lack of funds. The United States Government disbursed four times as much for returning slaves to the coast as for the enterprise within Liberia; from 1819 to 1869 it spent $2,338,000 on Liberia itself, but some $10,037,500 on returning slaves. The colonizing societies gathered some moneys, largely through churches, but what actually reached Liberia was meager. In forty-seven years, from 1819 to 1866, the American Colonization Society spent approximately $2,688,907.[10] Yet as late as even the 1930's, funds received from mission boards and various philanthropic organizations amounted to more than the total government revenue, which in 1933 dropped as low as $321,000. This explains why for a long time Liberia depended largely upon Churches and missions to provide schools and medical facilities.

MODERN TIMES

After World War I, Britain held a monopoly of the world's sources of natural rubber. Overnight the price of rubber rose from 14¢ to $1.23 a pound. This caused the United States to look for new sources of rubber. In 1923 a survey team sent out by the Firestone rubber company discovered that Liberia was ideal for raising rubber trees. By 1926 the company had negotiated a ninety-nine-year lease on up to a million acres of land. In return for the use of the land, Firestone agreed to pay the government 6¢ per acre per year and 1 per cent of the price of all rubber sold. On this basis Liberia was able to secure a

[9] *Ibid.*, p. 2.
[10] *The Foreign Policy of the United States in Liberia* (New York: Pageant Press, 1957), p. 9.

$5,000,000 loan, and the country began to stabilize and gain self-confidence.[11]

Firestone developed only 200,000 of the million acres, and its total investment fell short of that projected. But it was still the largest rubber operation in the world, and it was there for everyone to see, from the unschooled tapper to the head of state—demonstrating that Liberia had resources which could be developed for the benefit of the whole nation.

One who saw this and understood clearly what it could mean for his country was William V. S. Tubman. When he became President in 1944, his administration began a concentrated effort to encourage the continued economic growth of the nation. The new approach is summed up in what is known as the open-door policy. In general, this means that the door is open to any foreign company that will invest capital and trained personnel to develop Liberia. It has also meant new legislation to remove discriminatory tax and labor laws, making Liberia one of the most attractive investment climates in all Africa.[12]

If the companies have profited, so has the country. In 1941 government revenues from all sources totaled a million dollars. In 1962 they amounted to $50 million.[13] Few modern nations can match this increase of 5,000 per cent in just twenty years. The new wealth has made possible all-weather roads into the interior, expansion of health programs, and the multiplication of schools even in villages where roads have not yet reached. These developments make Liberia even more attractive for further investment.

The most exciting economic development is the discovery of vast iron deposits which rank among the richest in the world. The Bomi Hills mine, which started production in 1956, and the Liberia-American-Swedish Mining Company at Mt. Nimba near the Guinea border, which began to produce ore in 1963, have made iron the largest Liberian export, surpassing even rubber.

Recently a domestic economic policy called Operation Pro-

[11] Marinelli, *op. cit.*, pp. 45-46.
[12] *Ibid.*, pp. 72-78.
[13] *Ibid.*, p. 76.

duction has been formulated to complement the open-door policy. Manufactured goods not produced in Liberia must, of
course, be obtained from abroad. But it is wasteful to spend
scarce cash for imports which could be produced better and
more cheaply at home. For example, no self-respecting Liberian
would eat the insipid, imported rice if he could get the flavor-
ful and more nourishing home-grown variety. Yet every year
the country spends millions of dollars on products such as rice,
which can be raised in Liberia, because the farmers do not
produce enough. Operation Production encourages Liberians to
produce all they can and save the trade balance for goods not
made domestically.

Stirring changes are taking place in Liberia, affecting every
phase of life. These occur in the providence of God and have
meaning for both the temporal and the spiritual welfare of men.
God is at work, and the Church must have a bold, farsighted
plan to carry out her mission to make disciples—a plan as
revolutionary in its own sphere as those being proposed in the
fields of public instruction, public health, business, and commerce.

CHAPTER II

THE PEOPLE

About 90 per cent of the million inhabitants of Liberia are tribal Africans who live in their ancestral homes and farm the land, using many of the same methods that were used generations ago. There are sixteen major tribes, and most of the tribal people live in villages in the interior.

Along the coast in the settlements and towns live the descendants of the 13,000 immigrants from America. Immigration dropped off almost completely after the American Civil War. Along with these two groups there are also the descendants of more than 5,000 persons from slave ships which, after the slave trade had been outlawed in 1808, were apprehended at sca and forced to turn their captives loose at some point on the coast of Africa.

The settlers who came from America called themselves Americo-Liberians to distinguish themselves from the tribesmen, whom they referred to as "aborigines." The recaptured slaves were called "Congos." They were tribal people from other parts of Africa; cut off from their own tribal life, they gravitated toward the society of the Americo-Liberians rather than to that of the hostile Liberian tribes. Whatever the original meaning of "Congo" and "Americo-Liberian," these terms are much less useful in modern Liberia. Yet they are used in the common parlance, and various groups in Liberia employ them with slightly different shades of meaning. Today the term Americo-Liberian might be thought a misnomer, since one would take it to refer only to someone who himself came from America. However, the children of these immigrants felt an even greater necessity to differentiate themselves from the tribal Africans, and so retained the name. Over the years the meaning has been broadened, until today it is a cultural term referring to anyone who has adopted the social customs of the Americo-Liberians.

Modern Liberian society has stratifications, but the lines

between one social level and the next are not sharply drawn. Since there was never a color bar and intermarriage diluted the bloodline distinctions, the level and degree of education, type of English spoken, and degree of adoption of Western ways are the criteria of stratification in the social order. For the purpose of this church growth study, the social structure may be divided into four main classes: the elite, the tribal peasants, the tribal wage earners, and the English literates. Churches and missions are growing and serving within all four.

THE ELITE

The upper stratum of Liberian society is a cultured elite. This group is a privileged class, with prestige in the eyes of its fellow citizens and great influence in the total society. For convenience we shall continue to call it the elite although this term is not in common use locally. The group was formerly limited to the America-Liberians and their descendants, but although being born into the right family certainly helps in Liberia, heritage is no longer the main factor determining whether a person will belong to the elite or be excluded from it. Those with tribal background, if suitably educated, are also elite.

A college education, comfortable financial circumstances, and a high level of cultural achievement mark the members of this upper group. English is their mother tongue, and to belong, one must speak it fluently and impeccably. Most of the elite trace their ancestry back to the original settlers, but nearly all can claim a tribal ancestor or two when occasion calls for it. In 1960, fourteen out of thirty-one members of the House of Representatives were of tribal background, and so were two out of ten in the Senate. The tribal ratio is higher now.

The elite rule Liberia, not only because a large number of them are employed in government service or hold public office, but also because they set the social pattern in everything from dress style to currently acceptable ideas and opinions. Through their knowledge of English they know the world situation and naturally fill the leadership positions in the country. These are the Liberians who have taken advantage of whatever education was available. Until recently this was principally in schools of the Church and mission. Many of them have studied abroad in America or Europe, and all seek the best possible education for their children, recognizing it as the touchstone of opportunity.

Aside from government service, they work as lawyers, bankers, and businessmen. Foreign businessmen are anxious to have members of the elite as partners in their firms. This not only lends prestige to any operation but insures against prejudicial treatment or harassment from petty government officials. Many of the elite own their own rubber, coffee, or cocoa farms, from which they realize a more or less steady income. However, some of these operations are too small to be profitably carried on with labor paid at the current rate. Laborers conscripted from the villages by political friends, or sent by a chief in lieu of money to pay a fine, are available to work on these marginal farms.[1] Some have inherited urban land from their parents, the value of which has multiplied many times in a few years. More recently, the elite are those who have had capital and the understanding to take advantage of preferred stock offerings and other investments which the concessions have opened to Liberian citizens at attractive rates.

The elite marry within their own stratum of society. The old, established families of Monrovia are all interrelated through marriage. The women are especially unwilling to marry beneath their station; the men are less bound by this pattern. Most of Liberia's elite live in and around Monrovia, where the government offices are concentrated. Some live in the other coastal settlements: Cape Palmas, Harper, Cape Mount. Except for the few younger men who are employed in administrative positions by the concessions or in government positions in the former provinces, almost none of the elite live in the tribal areas of the interior.

This isolation, both cultural and geographical, has always been a major factor in the slow spread of Christianity from the elite, who are Christians, to the tribes of the hinterland. Though

[1] *Changing Liberia, a Challenge to the Christian,* Report of the United Christian Fellowship Conference of Liberia, July 1958 (Monrovia: Phelps-Stokes Fund, 1959), p. 63.

they have not spread their religion effectively among the tribal people, the elite play an active and prominent role in the life of the churches in the communities where they live. Some serve as part-time pastors of local congregations. Many are third- and fourth-generation Christians. The overwhelming majority hold membership in one of the older Protestant Churches: Baptist, Methodist, or Episcopalian.

The elite is not a closed society. Any Liberian who has the money, position, education, and cultural finesse, or an abundance of any one of these distinctions, may be included. With the rapid expansion of the Liberian economy, and as money and education are available to an ever-increasing number in the population, this uppermost class will expand, and the distance between it and the next-lower stratum of society will diminish. Already the elite are not so elite. This social change is taking place faster than most Liberians can adjust to it. However, for the foreseeable future the elite will remain the functioning upper-class stratum of Liberian society.

TRIBAL PEASANTS

At the other end of the social spectrum are the tribal peasants who live in the villages of the interior and farm the lands of their ancestral homes. I deal with them next because one must see them clearly in order to understand the orientation and motivation of the middle strata of Liberian society. Tribal peasants are most significant for our study, since the rapid expansion of the Church that characterizes people movements is very likely in this tribal stratum of the population. The sixteen major tribes are separate and distinct, each with its own language and customs. Relatively few anthropological studies have been made of these tribes of the Liberian hinterland, so that a general survey is impractical. Several authors have described each tribe in epigrammatic paragraphs; this kind of writing is a disservice to the people of Liberia, since such statements are often derogatory and, like similar generalizations about races and nationalities, mostly false, or at least partly so.

The map on page 31 was drawn in 1947 and is the best available to the writer to indicate the distribution of tribes and

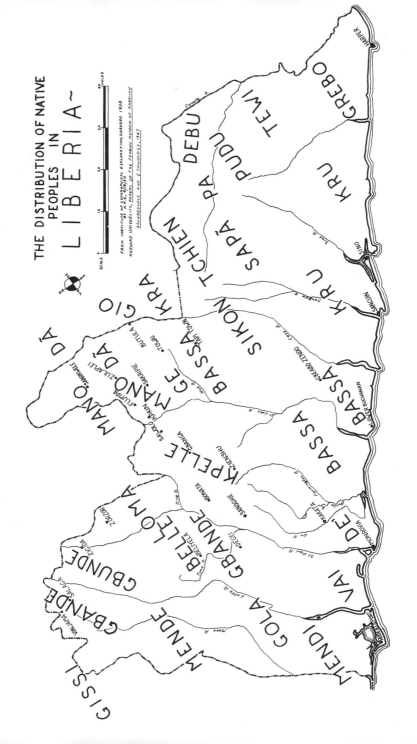

THE DISTRIBUTION OF NATIVE
PEOPLES IN
LIBERIA~

SCALE

MILES
0   10   20   30   40

FROM INSTITUTE OF GEOGRAPHICAL EXPLORATION, HARVARD, 1938
BY H. E. W. MANSO
HARVARD UNIVERSITY, PAPERS OF THE PEABODY MUSEUM OF AMERICAN
ARCHAEOLOGY AND ETHNOLOGY, 1947

subtribes. However, in the last twenty years there has been much additional penetration of the hinterland, and there has always been great variation in the English spelling of these names and places, so that both place names and tribal names and locations on this 1947 map may not always coincide exactly with the text.

The following description of the Loma tribe is based on four years' experience as a missionary in that tribe, including fifteen months of concentrated language study. I tender it as true and correct for the Loma and substantially true for most other tribes of the interior. Any reader familiar with the culture of another Liberian tribe will recognize many similarities as well as some differences. In any case, the culture of other tribes is more like that of the Loma than it is like the culture of the Americo-Liberians or a tribe on another continent.

An estimated 50,000 Lomas live in Liberia in the relatively mountainous region along the Guinea border between Zorzor and the Lofa River. This includes the three "clans" of the Gizema, Buliama, and Ziema. (Anthropologically speaking it is inexact to use the term clan to describe these divisions of the Loma tribe since they are a geographical and political grouping of villages. Technically speaking, the word clan refers to a division based on kinship.) The two northern clans between the Lofa River and Voinjama are referred to as the Gbunde tribe, but are actually only different "clans" of the Loma tribe. Their language has dialectical differences from the Loma of the three clans, but these are small, so that even a foreign speaker of Loma like myself can understand and be understood by them. The Loma tribe extends into Guinea, and many of the Loma in Liberia have relatives in Guinea.

According to Loma folk histories, "our mother was a Mandingo" (a Muslim tribe) and "we migrated to Liberia from the north."[2] The first migrations must have taken place more than a hundred years ago, since there are hundred-year-old

[2] George Schwab and George W. Harley, *Tribes of the Liberian Hinterland,* "Papers of the Peabody Museum of American Archaeology and Ethnology," Vol. XXXI (Cambridge, Mass.: Harvard University Press, 1947), p. 28.

cottonwood or bombax trees at several town sites, planted to remind the illiterate citizens of treaties and agreements made in the times of intertribal wars.

Several Loma towns have more than three hundred huts.* This is somewhat larger than the towns of most other tribes in Liberia. In the time of war the large towns afforded better protection from raiding Mandingo warriors. They were well fortified, with high walls and gates. Sections of the old packed-earth walls can still be seen at Yiella on the Guinea border, standing twenty-two feet high.

A typical Loma house is a round, windowless dwelling of one room. It has a conical roof thatched with palm fronds. In more recent times rectangular multiroomed houses with windows have been built. Corrugated iron roofing lasts longer than the thatch and has status symbol value as well. It is widely used even in towns some hours' walk from the road. Almost all the houses with iron roofs are rectangular.

The walls of the houses are constructed by lashing poles in vertical position all around the house at three or four inch intervals. These supports are cross-laced with bamboo and vine, and plastered with mud. A goat-walk collar made of tamped earth strengthens the base of the walls. When the mud is dry, the walls are daubed with white chalk inside and out, and the lower half of the walls and floor is rubbed with cow dung. Sometimes the white exterior walls are decorated with charcoal and red laterite pictures and designs. The houses are not arranged in any particular order or at any particular angle in the village. Sometimes the wider paths and drainage ditches will form crooked streets of a type, but except in the larger towns with motor road connections, none of these paths would allow a motor vehicle to pass. The women keep the space between the houses bare of all

---

* Sooner or later the reader may be puzzled by the almost interchangeable use, in this volume, of the words *village* and *town* for named places in the tribal areas. Nor is this surprising. The fact is that the two terms do not have the same mutually exclusive meaning, defined by mere number of inhabitants or houses, as would be true in Europe or America. All tribal settlements *look* like—and are—villages; yet in Liberia they are called towns.

grass and weeds as a precaution against stepping on snakes at night, or invasion of the houses by driver ants.

A Loma man builds a large round house for the women and children of his family, and a smaller house across a courtyard for himself. In the large houses packed earthen shelves for sleeping are built around the room against the wall. Western-style wooden beds with slats are common in the men's houses and in the rectangular ones; in the latter the whole family sleeps under the same roof, in different rooms.

The women cook on the fire in the middle of their house or in an open-sided kitchen behind it. Rice and tools are stored in the attics of these kitchens. Many families enclose the cooking kitchen and house with a bamboo or mud fence. The women tend small vegetable gardens at the edge of town. These are fenced to keep livestock out, since cows, goats, sheep, ducks, and chickens, and in some towns pigs, wander at will through the streets.

Most families have another house in the forest a few miles from the town, near the place where they make their farm. Sometimes eight or ten of these farmhouses are built in a single clearing to form a "half-town."

Rice is the staple of the Loma diet, and rice farming is the basis of the agricultural economy. This is carried out by what is known to agriculture as the slash-and-burn method. The farming cycle begins in December with the selection of a forest site and ends with the harvest in October. Members of both sexes take part, but there is strict division of labor. The farms range in size from three to ten acres depending on the number of wives, family members, and friends who can be counted on to help with the work.

After the site has been approved by the chief and elders of the village, the men spend two or three weeks cutting the vines and underbrush. The cutlass, a knife with a blade about two feet long and a slight hook on the end, and a rawhide glove for the left hand, are the implements used. A month or so after this first "underbrushing" the men spend another two weeks cutting the larger trees. An axe is used to supplement the cutlass at this stage. The stumps are left waist-high. When the brush and trees are dry enough, and preferably after a rain, the farm is burned over. Half a dozen men with long split-bamboo torches held like spears race through the tangle, and plunging their torches into the dry material set it aflame. On a favorable day in March a dozen fires or more may be seen from a single village. It takes another week to gather the unburned branches and sticks into small piles and burn them. The larger logs are left where they lie.

Until now only the men have been involved; when the burning is finished the women take over. After the first rains, when the weed seeds are well sprouted, they begin "scratching the farm." Rice seed, mixed with corn and sometimes millet, is sown broadcast in the immediate area. Then the women, bending over at the waist, cultivate the area sown, using a hoe with a blade two inches wide on a handle eighteen inches long, cutting weeds and covering the seed rice in a single process. Thus the farm is finished. The children are sent daily into the field for a week or two to frighten away the birds until the seeds sprout.

Before the fruit of their labor is realized, it may be necessary to fence the whole farm to protect the young plants from groundhogs. To do this, three-foot lengths of stick are split and sharpened and driven into the ground side by side at an angle slanting out, to enclose the farm. There is no protection against deer except the hunter's gun.

The women harvest the ripened grain in October, using a small knife with a blade an inch and a half long. Every stalk of grain is cut individually between thumb and knife. When she has a handful of stalks the woman ties them into a bundle with a rice straw, and lays the little sheaf on a nearby stump. At the end of the day the sheaves are stacked in piles, and later removed to the attics for storage.

To prepare rice for a meal a woman takes two or three sheaves from the attic, still tied with the rice straw, and treads out the grain with her feet on a mat. When most of it is off, she shreds each stalk between thumb and forefinger so as not to miss a single precious grain. She then puts the rice in a wooden mortar and pounds off the husks with a pole five or six feet long and separates the chaff from the grain by tossing it up in a flat fanner basket. By the time it is washed and put in the iron pot bubbling over the fire, a great deal of care and energy has been expended on each grain. Those who accuse Africans of laziness ought to have the experience of trying to keep up with these Loma farmers at work—male or female.

The men climb the tall oil palms and cut down the bunches of palm nuts. The red oil and palm butter extracted from the outside of the nut are used extensively in the Loma cuisine. After the nuts have been dried, a woman uses a large stone for an anvil and cracks them with a smaller stone to get out the kernels. A bushel of kernels is worth about $1.50 in the shop of a Lebanese trader. Palm nuts are a major source of cash for the Loma family. Some coffee and cocoa are also raised and sold for cash.

Fruits and vegetables commonly grown include cassava, several varieties of plantains and bananas, pineapple, okra, pepper, eddoes, squash, yams, sweet potatoes, cucumbers, onions, and avocados. The heart of a certain palm is cut and the sweet juice collected and fermented to make palm wine. Sugar cane is raised, and the juice fermented and distilled to make a cane rum.

Two types of cotton are grown. The women remove the seeds, card and spin the cotton, and dye the thread. Using narrow looms, the men weave the thread into six-inch strips of cloth which they then sew together. All sewing is done by men. Some in nearly every village work as tailors using treadle sewing machines. The men wear the *tokobai* or chief's robe made of country cloth over their pants. The women wear a kind of breechcloth made of this coarse country cloth as an undergarment. Their outer garment, the *lappa*, consists of a single piece of cloth some two yards long, wrapped around the body under the arms, or sometimes at the waist. They carry their children on their backs, wrapped inside the *lappa*.

Other work reserved strictly for women is the weaving of soft mats and raffia bags, and making round fish nets and fishing with them. The women's musical instrument is a gourd rattle made with beads strung on the outside.

Loma men build their own houses, but in every village there are sawyers who specialize in sawing logs into planks in the forest, and carpenters who build doors, doorjambs, and window sills. Specialists are hired to put the corrugated iron roofs on new houses. The blacksmiths have a well-organized, powerful guild. In every town they sit in their sheds beside bellow-fanned charcoal fires, making cutlasses and knives and carving wooden stools and mortars. Blacksmiths are the keepers of the special knives used by the *poro* society for scarification and circumcision. They and their apprentices are exempt from conscription for public work such as repairing bridges and cutting the brush along the paths and roads.

Other work reserved strictly for men includes weaving baskets and heavy mats, all the hunting and trapping and making the traps, butchering and skinning domestic animals. The men's musical instruments are the *y*-shaped harp or lyre (*kwinegi*), drums of various kinds, and horns made from elephant tusks and cow horns.

The basic farming unit is the household, which includes not only the head and his wife and children, but also any kinsmen or friend who resides in his house. A man's obligations for work extend beyond the limits of his own family. If his old father is still alive, he will join his brothers and sisters in "making farm" for him. His father-in-law, his nearest neighbors in the quarter, and his mother's oldest brother may all expect him to help them with their farm work, and he is obliged to render such service. He is also obliged to help make the chief's farm and that of the chief blacksmith. He may contract financial agreements or be involved in marriage arrangements that obligate him to yet others in the community. He is not bound to do the work himself, but may send a son or someone who for some reason owes him a debt of farm work. For example, in the Loma town of Zorzor, on the day appointed by the congregation for working on the church's farm, a number of members of the congregation who were employed sent 50¢ each by a messenger explaining that they had other work that day. This illustrates the fact that the promise of participating in cooperative work is thought of as a real debt that must be paid. The person whose farm is being worked is responsible for feeding the workers.

The obligation of a man toward his kin group is taken very seriously. It is most important to be present at the burial of any relative. Foreign employers are often shocked at the amount of time an employee must spend attending the funerals and settling the estates of his relatives. The strength of these kinship ties has important implications for the growth of the churches among this segment of the Liberian population.

The religion of the Loma tribesmen, commonly referred to as animism, is a kind of ancestor spirit worship. The individual is responsible to the larger community, which includes forebears both living and dead. Participation in the corporate life of this community is the core of the religious experience. Breaking a vow or offending a dead ancestor can have as dire a consequence as breaking a taboo or custom of the living community. If a person pleases and honors the spirits of his ancestors, they will protect and even help him. If sickness and misfortune befall him, it is because he has offended someone. This may be a member of the living community who is now bewitching or even poisoning him; or he may have offended a spirit in the community of his ancestors.

In either case, the procedure is to discover who has been offended and do something to make amends. In the case of a member of the living community, it may be enough to beg forgiveness or make a token present. Loma religion has no set times for ritual or worship such as those in Christianity or Islam; sacrifices are made and ritual participated in only when the need arises. For example, in the village of Wozi, after two hunting accidents had occurred within a month, every man in the village participated in a ritual washing, and the blood of a sacrificial goat was sprinkled over special offerings and fetishes to ward off further misfortune.

On the individual level, for example, if a child sickens unexpectedly, the mother will first go to a "sand player" (diviner), often a Mandingo trader, to discover what—or rather who—is afflicting her child. The sand player observes the pattern formed by bones (or bottle caps) cast on the ground and prescribes proper remedial action. It is not unusual for him to demand that the woman confess an illicit love affair or other trespass before he will agree to help her. Then he may tell her to kill a chicken and sprinkle the blood and feathers on cola nuts placed on the grave of her recently deceased mother or some other ancestor whose spirit is cursing the child. Or, in some cases, he will direct her to a *zo* (witch doctor), who can make medicine for this particular illness and protect the child from further harm and from the further influence of a witching spirit, living or dead. In some instances, if the symptoms are readily recognizable, the mother may go directly to a *zo* who has a reputation for curing that particular illness.

The *zo*'s are people said to be possessed of the power to heal or help. Until the coming of Western medicine the *zo* was the only source of comfort to whom the stricken villager could turn. Some bonesetters and herbalists had actual medical relief to offer as well as psychological comfort. There are many varieties and degrees of *zo* power. For example, a young man who had *zo* power over snakes (many of which are poisonous in Liberia) jumped from the jeep he was riding in after it ran over a snake in the road. Unafraid, he pursued it into the thick underbrush beside the road and killed it. His companions, both older than he, cowered in the car. Some *zo*'s also have power to counteract the charms and spells of witches who are poisoning or thought to be poisoning a person. Even a *zo* of mediocre power can come up with a love potion or a good luck charm.

The Loma tribe is one of many in West Africa in which secret societies, *poro* for the men and *sande* for the women, have a dominant influence. Both the *sande* and *poro* cults hold bush schools, which are institutions for the instruction of the young members of the tribe. These schools at the same time conduct initiation ceremonies for the secret society. Death is the penalty for betrayal of its secrets.[3]

A session of the bush school is held alternately by the *poro* and the *sande* societies every seven years, so that a school of boys graduates every fourteen years. Formerly the initiates spent much of the full seven years in the bush school in an isolated camp in the forest with the *zo*'s, but in modern times very few of the boys actually live in the bush school for more than a few months. The government has not forbidden the *poro* and *sande* cults to hold their schools, but the length of time has been strictly regulated so that no child who is in regular school will be kept from class because of participation in initiation

---

[3] *Ibid.*, p. 274.

rites. Many schoolboys pay the fee, enter, and leave the bush
school within the three-month school vacation period, barely
long enough for the scarification marks to heal. These marks
are cut on the chest, back, and neck of the initiates while they
are in the *poro* bush. The rows of scars represent teeth marks,
and the boys are said to have been chewed and swallowed by
the "big thing" in the forest. Some instruction in handicrafts
and customs of the tribe also takes place in the bush school, but
a majority of the initiates remain too short a time to learn
much. Also, many children enter it when they are under three
years of age and too young to learn.

Living in isolation in the forest, away from the care of their
mothers, for a period of several months is hazardous. Young
children frequently die. No one is allowed to leave and seek
medical assistance, nor is any doctor or nurse allowed to come
to the bush school. Infant mortality, already high in Loma
villages, skyrockets during the bush school sessions for initiates. In Fisebu in 1963, 11 boys died out of a total of 123 who
went into the school.

The *sande* society initiation poses special health hazards for
the women of the tribe. Not only are the scarification, cliteri-
dectomy, and female circumcision with unsterile knives danger-
ous in themselves, but the complications in childbirth that are
the direct result of this latter operation contribute substantially
to the infant mortality rate.

Zo's who are the leaders of the *poro* and *sande* societies are
referred to as "devils." The "Big Devil" or Grand Master is
never seen by any but the initiated and is said to remain always
in the forest. It is forbidden to members of the opposite sex to
know or say his actual name. In fact, he lives in the village and
goes about his business of farming or blacksmithing like any
other man, when not involved in rituals of the society. Lesser
devils sometimes appear in the village to dance on special
occasions. These men are dressed in raffia skirts and leggings
that completely conceal their person. They wear black carved
wooden masks on their heads. Though they are Lomas, these
dancers speak Kpelle—which has prestige—in a singsong
falsetto voice. Special music made by blowing across the mouth
of empty jugs and the sound of the bull-roarer and special bells

are said to be the voice of the Big Devil.[4] The head *zo* in the society, and the society as a corporate whole, exert absolute influence over individual members. The individual rarely if ever contradicts the action of the society.

In 1964 the government of Liberia abolished the distinction between the provinces of the interior and the counties along the coast, and a county system was inaugurated throughout the country. The chief executive in each county is the superintendent, who is appointed by the President. Two senators, and representatives according to the number of voters, are elected in each county. In the hinterland and wherever along the coast the population is mainly tribal, the government rules through the tribal system. The national government has supremacy over tribal government, but the tribal chief is the instrument by which the national government communicates information and policies to the tribal people. The chief also serves the government in labor recruitment and in the collection of taxes.[5] In 1905 a law was passed by the Liberian legislature providing for the election of chiefs.

The highest official within the tribal government is the paramount chief. This office is not indigenous to the original Loma culture, but has been adapted from elsewhere in Liberia.[6] Beneath him are the clan chiefs and town or village chiefs. The towns are divided into subdivisions called quarters, each with a quarter chief. Heads of families are responsible for members of their immediate households. Courts exist at every level and have their respective jurisdictions. Marital strife, so long as it is just a family problem, is often settled at a family council or moot, with representatives present from the families of both wife and husband. Land disputes may be settled in the town chief's court or a clan chief's court. More important matters, such as divorce, larceny, assault, or murder, will be immediately referred to higher levels for decision. The govern-

[4] Pierre Dominique Gaisseau, *Forêt Sacrée: Magie et Rites Secrets des Toma* (Paris: A. Michel, 1953), p. 112.

[5] Henry B. Cole, ed., *The Liberian Yearbook, 1962* (Monrovia: Liberian Review Publication, 1962), p. 56.

[6] Schwab and Harley, *op. cit.*, p. 165.

ment's policy is to permit tribal law to operate so long as it does not interfere with national policy.[7]

The Loma have strong tribal laws against stealing. In the isolated village of Wozi, when I was on language study, my wife and I often left for the weekend without locking the doors of our house. Nothing was ever missing when we returned. In this case tribal and national law dovetail nicely. In some other matters a basic conflict exists.

TRIBAL WAGE EARNERS

The tribal wage earners are men who have left their homes in the interior to seek work in urban centers, plantations, and at new industrial sites. They have grown up in the tribal village and still have strong ties to tribal institutions. Their mother tongue is one of the tribal languages, but they speak and understand a little pidgin English which they have picked up on their own.

The main reason they leave home is to earn money. Even in the Loma village there are demands for cash. A man needs money when the hut tax is due, or to put a zinc roof on his house, or to pay a debt or the dowry for a wife. For many men the easiest and quickest way to acquire money is to go down toward the coast, get a job, and work until the money is raised. These are "target" workers. Some who have the skill to earn forty dollars a month become committed to the money economy, in the sense that they no longer "make" a farm. They remain more or less permanently in their new locations, yet retain their ties with their villages, going home to "buy" a wife or when a relative dies. They send their children back to attend bush school. All plan to return to the village some day, when they are old, or if they come upon hard times.

The less fortunate workers who labor for ten to fifteen dollars a month at unskilled tasks usually return home during the

[7] Johnetta Cole, "Notes on Traditional Occupations and Work Patterns of Tribal Liberians," from "Northwestern University Economic Survey of Liberia" (Evanston, Ill., 1962), p. 10. Staff paper, mimeographed; to be published.

farming season[8]; many of these save their money with a specific goal in mind. When they have enough, they go home. The Firestone plantation tried raising wages in an effort to stabilize this seasonal mobility and rapid turnover of the labor force. But the higher wages had just the opposite effect. The workers achieved their goals (targets) and departed all the sooner. Stability in the work force is achieved by providing better housing, so that the worker's family can join him. A man living with his wife and children is more permanent than a single man.

Another reason the men themselves give for leaving their villages is to escape "porter work." In a Loma village, since the people have little cash, some of their taxes are contributed in the form of labor on public works. They cut brush along the paths and work on community farms, from which the harvest goes for taxes, and carry loads for officials and soldiers traveling in the area. The burden of porter work would not be heavy if shouldered equally by all members of the community, but in every town some men are exempt. Naturally the chiefs and quarter chiefs are spared porter work. Powerful zo's and their helpers are exempt. Blacksmiths and their apprentices are exempt. Ex-soldiers are exempt, and one friend each, too. Those to whom the chief owes money are also likely to be exempt. Thus, when it comes right down to carrying the load, porter work falls to a few old men and the unestablished youngsters. The young men leave by the dozens as soon as they are able. Many Loma men join the army for a few years and thus get perpetual immunity from public works. Others stay away for varying periods of time.

Gerald Currens has described well the situation in which these people find themselves when they leave their village:

> In these urban and industrial areas, people of all kinds and with varied tribal backgrounds are thrown together in compulsory community without the familiar basis for community. Distrust, loneliness, easily abused freedom, all thrive in such an environment. Diversity in language and customs is a barrier to communal life, and the transient mentality mili-

[8] Henry B. Cole, *loc. cit.*

tates against any feeling of responsibility toward the community.

Fortunately, in most company camps friends and even relatives may be near; usually a person goes to a place where there is a member of his family or an acquaintance. In the urban areas natural grouping into tribal neighborhoods takes place . . . witness Loma Town in Monrovia or the Loma and Kpelle quarters in Vai Town (Bomi Hills). At Firestone, a Kpelle or Loma headman at a division camp will draw laborers of his tribe to that camp.

But the old patterns of life are disrupted and new ones take shape. The sanctions of tribal society and the control of family or elders are no longer effectual. Yet there are vestiges of the familiar forms of community life. The tribal groups have their chiefs, who are recognized authorities in the community with quasi-legal functions. New groupings become dynamic social forces: one's fellow workers, the labor union, and of course where there is one, the Christian congregation.[9]

The tribal man in his home town or village, speaking his own language, is a man in his own right, respected, sure of himself and in complete control of the social situation, a different person entirely from the same man transported to an urban center or industrial area. In that situation he is a stranger, subject to unfamiliar laws, where his ability to speak well (of which a Loma man is very proud) is taken from him by his lack of knowledge of anything but the Loma tongue. His remarks are mistranslated by an interpreter with a haughty, superior attitude. Even a greying warrior must give place to a fresh schoolboy in the fourth grade. The tribal man away from his village home is a shell of his former self.

The women who follow their husbands into these areas, or are tempted by the bright lights of the city and the freedom from farm work, must make an even greater adjustment. In the tribal village the wife and mother is a producing and essential part of the family economy. In the urban areas everything must

[9] Gerald E. Currens, "Urban and Industrial Evangelism," study brochure for the Study Conference of the Evangelical Lutheran Church in Liberia (Monrovia, 1963), p. 17. Mimeographed.

be purchased, even wood, with the husband's wages. Many women (some 5,000 in Monrovia) engage in petty trading, sitting for hours in front of their houses or on the street with a few meager wares, making twenty-five to fifty cents for the day.[10] "Within the tribal community the woman maintains a certain economic and social independence. The loss of this and the lack of any satisfying role leads to the disruption of family life, to hasty divorce and prostitution."[11]

The Church has only begun to minister to the tribal wage earners. One by one, some few are won to the Church, but conversions are slow and fragile. The men seem preoccupied with other things. As one Lutheran evangelist, Peter Giddings, working in the mine community of Bomi Hills, said, "They all have their own business to attend to, and that is always most important. The people who come here are different from those in the bush. Those who come here, come for only one thing—to make money."[12]

That the Church should gather these displaced tribal wage earners into congregations goes without saying, but church growth back home in their tribal villages will be the strongest, most effective means of evangelism among them. They regard their wage-earning situation as temporary, and are unwilling to make a major religious decision apart from their tribal community. But when a man's kinship group in his home village becomes Christian, he too will seek baptism. Furthermore, where there is a strong congregation in the village, young men often seek out the pastor and ask to be baptized before they "go down" for the first time, feeling the need for a stronger relationship with God in their new venture. Those who leave the village as Christians are much more likely to attend church in their new environment than those who regard the Church as a part of the foreignness of the new place.

[10] George Dalton, "The Dilemma of Piecemeal Change in Tribal Life," from "Northwestern University Economic Survey of Liberia" (Evanston, Ill., 1962), p. 8. Staff paper, mimeographed; to be published.

[11] Currens, *op. cit.*, p. 19.

[12] *Ibid.*, p. 21.

ENGLISH LITERATES

In the fluid stream of society in Liberia, the English literates form the stratum that moves with the swiftest current. In local parlance they are sometimes referred to as the "civilized element." They are the "civilized" sons and daughters of tribal parents, people on their way up who have most to gain from the vast social changes that are sweeping Liberia. They are not afraid of new ways or ideas, as their parents were. As a group, they have made an almost conscious choice of change as a way of life. If they err, it will not be because they resisted the forces of change, but because they adopted indiscriminately any new thing that came along simply because it was new. They place great faith in the power of education to lift up the masses as they themselves have been lifted up, and they have an almost idolatrous trust of the school as the source of every good thing.

They are in a hurry to forget their own tribal past and its culture and adopt everything Western, the good with the bad. Anxious to speak English, they would willingly forget their acquaintance with one of the native languages. They studiously copy the life and culture of the elite. For example, they may casually mention that they boil their drinking water in the presence of someone they think will appreciate this sign of enlightened fastidiousness.

Individuals in this group are fighting hard not to return to what they consider a lower level in society, and they work overtime to achieve a position at a higher status level. But as the world, and especially Africa, begins to accept things African, and an appreciation of the tribal heritage emerges, the English literates develop a certain ambivalence toward their cultural background.

When Loma boys go to school, for example, they take a "civilized" name. If they change schools or graduate they will often change their name again. It is common for a boy to have four or more names in the course of his school career. Indicative of the growing acceptance of things African is the fact that, although between grade school and high school students often adopt purely Western names, between high school and college—or at graduation from college—a number of them take a name with at least one element that indicates tribal origin. Many educated men introduce themselves in a way that indicates their pride in it; thus, "My name is John Freeman, Grebo by tribe." Others, on the other hand, are reticent about it; they speak perfect English and make unconcealed references to their experiences in a college abroad, so that one would assume they were not of tribal background if one did not know.

This is the stratum of society that has the education and skills to fill salaried positions as teachers, clerks, lower-echelon government positions, and minor supervisory posts in industry. Many of the full-time pastors in the churches are in this category. Nurses and medical technicians mostly come from this group.

There is a fairly large church membership among the English literates, and their marriage ideals are those of Christianity and the elite, but in practice they are strongly influenced by the more promiscuous tribal standards. On the other hand, some are almost Victorian in attitude, seeing this not only as the proper expression of their Christian life, but also as a way of asserting their right to a position at a higher level in Liberian society.

English literates live where demand for their skills and education are greatest. Monrovia and the urban centers attract the majority. An increasing number are living at the industrial sites, and as more skilled positions are required in the trade centers of the interior villages, they will move to fill those positions. At present, the few who do return to the interior wield a great influence among their people. They are much more effective agents of social change than the foreign missionaries, for example.

The rapid expansion of the public school system is providing an ever-increasing segment of the population with education, which is the means of access to this stratum of society. School population has risen from 24,000 in 1950 to 61,000 in 1961.[13] Education is the door of opportunity; the society is open-ended, and the sky is the limit. I have heard a teacher in the public

[13] Dalton, *op. cit.*, p. 3.

school of a tiny Loma village urge his students to greater industry with the challenge: "One of you might grow up to be Secretary of State, or even President one day." And he is right. It is a real possibility.

A danger in the present situation is that barely skilled or partly trained people will be added to Liberian society faster than the economy can absorb them. Even three years of schooling make a man unfit for rice farming or rubber tapping in the eyes of tribal people, yet so little schooling does not give him the skills or education to do much of anything else. With the high rate of dropout from schools, there are hundreds of young men in this situation. With their hopes unfulfilled, as they grow older and the door of opportunity closes, they easily take out their frustrations in antisocial activities. New light industry may provide jobs for some, but only a new attitude toward the dignity of labor can free most of them to go back to the agricultural tasks that are basic to Liberia's economic stability.

The English literates, anxious to be as completely Westernized as possible, very readily become Christians. However, thus far they have not carried Christianity back to their tribal relatives in the villages. Perhaps many think becoming Christian a cultural rather than a religious step. For the truly Christian, however, bringing their village kinsmen into the faith is the obvious next step. With a little sacrifice it is quite possible, and the urgency of it cannot be too much stressed.

THE FOUR MAIN CLASSES ACCORDING TO STATUS

The *elite,* at the upper end of the social spectrum, speak English as their mother tongue and have the advantages of education. The second stratum is that of the *English literates,* who, though they may speak English as well as the elite, and in some cases better, are from tribal stock or mixed parentage, and their social customs are slightly less Westernized. People at this level of society are trying to forget their tribal background and are on their way up. The third stratum is that of the *tribal wage earners.* These are men who have grown up speaking a tribal language but have left their village to seek employment in one of the industrial centers of the country. They speak a little

English, which for the most part they have picked up on their own. Very few are literate. Most of them fully intend to return some day to their ancestral homes, though circumstances may keep them in their new surroundings longer than they plan. Finally, the fourth stratum is that of the *tribal peasants.* They form the large majority of the population, still living and dying in the villages of their ancestors. They speak the language of their tribe and follow its culture patterns.

Still another stratum, which is not treated here, is made up of certain of the less educated citizens—some of tribal origin, some the descendants of English-speaking settlers, but all marked by lack of education. In many cases they live in small settlements isolated from the rapid currents of social and economic change that are sweeping Liberia.

Linguistic traits alone are not adequate to distinguish social groups and subgroups in this country; but the shift from tribal languages to English indicates the direction of cultural change. The degree and quality of English a person uses goes a long way to determine his social standing, and it has the added advantage of being a measurable culture trait.

UNIFICATION POLICY

In light of the wide divergence of these four social strata and the existence of sixteen different tribes, perhaps the greatest single achievement of the Tubman administration is not any material accomplishment—new roads or schools, or economic development—but the Unification Policy. This declaration that there is to be no more Americo-Liberianism as against tribalism is as important for the citizens of Liberia as the Supreme Court decision banning segregation in the schools is for citizens of the United States. Although there will still be instances of Americo-Liberian supremacy and pockets of tribal exclusiveness; nevertheless, unification is the policy. The law of the nation, which forms the mores of the future, is on the side of unity.

However, a very great barrier to unity in Liberia remains: the gulf between Christianity and paganism. As long as there are men whose lives are ruled by fear of fetishes, juju, and witch-craft, unification will be incomplete. Until those men move into the camp of those who fear the one true God and acknowledge Christ as Lord, a schism will remain that is greater than educa-tion or economic advance can bridge. It remains for the Churches to make disciples of the whole nation of Liberia. The government for its part has done a great deal. It is the church-men who are slow. Why are there still villages in which no one preaches the Gospel? Why are there still whole clans in which not a single church exists? Surely this cannot be the will of God! If the Churches and missions have been too busy running schools and clinics to fulfill their responsibilities for spiritual leadership, then it is time they recognized their primary obliga-tion. The government is establishing schools. The government is moving rapidly to provide medical care for all its citizens; but only the Churches will plant village congregations and nurture them. If they do not do it, if the Church does not win the souls of men—whole villages—to Christ, then Liberia will remain dismembered. Yet perhaps not, for there is another possible specter in the background, Islam. God forbid that the masses of this Christian nation should turn to Islam. But under the tremendous sociological pressures of the new Africa, *the masses will change!* They will turn to *some* unifying ideology. The old ancestor cult is not enough to hold men together in the new circumstances. If Christianity will not unite Liberia, then per-haps Islam will.

In effect, there are two Liberias: the civilized country of the elite and the literate as contrasted with the Liberia of the tribes and tribal wage earners. These two are poles apart, but moving swiftly into a time of dramatic encounter. The result must be unity, not collision. No wonder God is impatient for His ser-vants to be up and about the harvest.

The Church is the only social institution that spans the two Liberias. In spite of the prevailing diversity and forces of division, the unity that already exists in the Church gives rise to the hope that real unity is possible for the nation. The Church must continue to serve both Liberias—God commands it. With the zeal of an evangelist she must teach and baptize the tribal nations, planting churches in every village and town. For civilized Liberia, the Church must speak out with a prophetic voice against social evils and injustices where they exist. Only by doing both can she faithfully fulfill her calling.

CHAPTER III

GROWTH OF THE BAPTIST AND
METHODIST CHURCHES

THE BASIC PATTERN

From the first, the Churches recognized that there was a unique opportunity for Protestant missions in Liberia. In 1820 the Baptist Church, Methodist Church, and Protestant Episcopal Missionary Society were organized on board the ship *Elizabeth,* which brought the first settlers. The colony's strongest and best leaders were active churchmen, and not a few were ordained ministers. Many nations have vague deistic references to a Creator in their founding documents, but Liberia's Declaration of Independence in 1847 was specifically Christian. It referred to the "native" converts as proof that, "from us, feeble as we are, the light of Christianity has gone forth."[1] The mission activity of the Churches was not only possible in Liberia, but expected and outwardly encouraged.

The colonists no less than their supporters in the sending Churches in America envisioned Liberia as the hope of Africa, a beachhead for Christianity from which the Gospel could spread to the interior tribes of the Dark Continent. The colonization societies had as one of their primary aims the "civilization and Christianization" of Africa. Indeed, some even thought that "every immigrant to Africa is a missionary carrying with him credentials in the holy cause of civilization, religion and free institutions."[2] This was not the case. The vast majority of the colonists were most ordinary people, struggling to make a living in the hostile environment of an uncivilized land. Yet

[1] Harry H. Johnston, *Liberia* (London: Hutchinson & Co., 1906), p. 200.
[2] Quoted from a speech of Henry Clay, January 20, 1827 (Cason, "Growth of the Church in the Liberian Environment," p. 22). Note that full data for sources cited in an earlier chapter will be found in the Bibliography.

53

many churches and Christians made contributions to the colonization societies as if they were mission stations.

The Churches understood that their mission involved carrying the Gospel to the tribes. Every denomination made reaching
the tribes its aim. In 1835 two Baptist missionaries, the Rev.
William Mylne and Rev. William Crooker, began their missionary careers by studying the Bassa language at Millsburg, since
they had been "designated exclusively to the native Africans."
Episcopal missionary Rev. James Thompson, serving as secretary to the governor of the colony, wrote, "The natives are our
only hope." Another Episcopal missionary, Rev. Lancelot B.
Minor, wrote as he began work among the tribesmen: "There
cannot be a doubt but that this branch of the mission, the
colonist, imperiously demands our attention; nor can it be neg-
lected without detriment in more ways than one, yet believing
myself called of God to preach the Gospel to the heathen,
nothing short of it can render me contented."[3]

In 1836 the Foreign Committee of the Protestant Episcopal
Church instructed their missionary, Dr. Savage, as follows: "The
great aim of your mission is towards the native Africans." This
concern for the Liberian tribesmen, even to the exclusion of the
colonists, has been typical of the planning of mission societies
working in Liberia, not only in the early years but throughout
the history of the republic.

However, the Churches did not carry out this plan. Christianity did not spread among the tribal people. What Dr. Savage
did indicates the direction mission work was actually to take for
nearly a century. He "decided that improvement of the civilized
and moral condition of the colonists was the immediate task
because these immigrants could set an example for the natives."[4] Most missionaries of the Baptist, Methodist, Episcopal,
and Presbyterian Churches, like Dr. Savage, intended to evangelize the tribes, but in fact spent their time in the coastal
settlements with the colonists.

The strategy of these missionaries on the field was to use the

[3] Quoted from Hennings, *History of the African Mission* (*ibid.*,
p. 141).
[4] *Ibid.*, p. 140.

colonists as a stepping stone to evangelization of the tribes. But they never got past the stepping stone. The fact that both colonists and tribes were Negroes concealed from missionaries and board secretaries alike the magnitude of the social gulf that separated the English-speaking America-Liberians from the tribal people. The brief account of the Loma and the elite in the last chapter will have made the reader partially aware of these differences. There was almost no social contact between the two groups through which the Gospel could readily pass, and so the attempt to reach the tribes through the America-Liberians *class* failed. The result was that Christianity was isolated in a kind *barrier* of cultural box of civilized settlers along the coast. This social gulf, augmented by actual geographical isolation brought about by hostilities between tribes and settlers, effectively prevented the spread of Christianity to the tribes. The colonists lived in the settlements near the coast; they had obtained the land for these settlements through agreements with the tribal chiefs, but as Cason says,

> The tribal people did not think in terms of a permanent alienation of their land. Neither did they believe that the coming of the colonists marked the end of the slave trade or the renunciation of tribal rights to plunder any ship wrecked on the coast. When the colonists came to Cape Mesurado they were only allowed to occupy tiny Perseverance Island. Chief Boatswain championed their cause so that the settlers were finally able to occupy the Cape itself, but they almost lost the land and their lives in a battle with the combined forces of the tribes at the end of 1822. Further battles were fought in 1826, 1828, 1835, 1839 and 1843. The tribes were at times instigated and aided by the slave traders. The colonists were occasionally helped by the British or American Navy vessels. The Liberian government made a real effort to end the slave trade but lacked the power to enforce the western laws of the colony among the tribes of the coast.[5]

Liberia did not actually rule the tribes of the interior until after World War I. Roads were not extended until after World War II. Travel beyond the limits of the settlements in the

[5] *Ibid.*, p. 87.

early days was extremely risky, and living in the interior out of
the question. As long as the tribes were at war with one another
and occasionally with the colonists, even safe-conduct agreements could not be depended upon. Attempts to evangelize
were made only among the tribes nearest the settlements. Time
and time again, raids, burnings, and war stopped missionary
expansion to the tribes. As early as 1838 the Methodists proposed to go to Sinoe and Boporo, but even as close as this to
the settlements—20 miles—mission work was given up for fear
political difficulties with the tribes might hinder it.[6] Even in
1911, when the Disciples of Christ made a survey from the
railhead in Sierra Leone at Pendembu through Bolahun,
Zorzor, and down the St. Paul River, they decided that the
interior was still "inaccessible for mission work and that the
government was not opening the territory very rapidly."[7] And
as late as the 1920's mission stations farther inland than Dobli
Island had to be closed because of tribal unrest. Thus hostility
and resulting separation made any prolonged contact with the
Gospel difficult if not impossible for the masses of tribal people.

    A more subtle barrier to the spread of Christianity lay in the
easy identification of Christianity with civilization. "Those sent
by the Churches as well as those sent by the colonization
societies made little or no distinction between Christianity and
Western Civilization."[8] This easy identification of Christian
faith with a culture gave the tribesmen the impression that to
become a Christian one would have to desert his own tribe and
become a member of a different tribe, the tribe of the foreign
invaders. Christianity was the religion of the settlers. A pattern
was established, certainly, by which a person could become a
Christian, but mostly it involved acquiring the attributes of
Western civilization. To be a Christian one had to learn to
speak and read English, because the Christians had a holy book
in English. And to learn to read one had to go to the foreigners'
school. Even today, the general emphasis on the Bible makes it

[6] *Ibid.*, p. 122.
[7] *Ibid.*, p. 294.
[8] *Ibid.*, p. 28.

difficult for Protestants to imagine how a person can be a Christian and not know how to read. (A tacit requirement which of course would have been absurd and literally impossible in the time of Christ or the early Church, or even the Middle Ages and considerably later. That this particular skill is no measure of readiness to accept Christ—or to serve Him well—is something we are rather prone to forget.) In Liberia several denominations have made literacy one of the prerequisites of baptism.

By their unconscious attitude the Americo-Liberians contributed to this confusion between Christianity and civilization. In the little settlements precariously perched on the edge of hostile tribal territory, they had to protect themselves from extinction, and used Christianity to preserve their identity—a bulwark for their ideals and their culture. It became one of the marks of being an Americo-Liberian, which distinguished them from the tribal people. Their status as Christians was a kind of natural birthright, a part of being "civilized." To them it was incredible that an uncivilized tribesman, who could not even speak English, might be a Christian. Missionaries and Liberian pastors who felt called to go to the "natives" met with resistance from the settlers. Bishop Roberts expressed the view of most missionaries and ministers in 1873 when he said, "The most feasible method of promoting their [the natives'] interest in a religious as well as a political point of view is to sustain and strengthen the churches in the civilized portion of our country."[9] When mission societies in the United States sent funds specifically designated for work among the tribal people, the settlers were naturally jealous. After all, their own children needed an education too.

The missionaries perpetuated the not uncommon confusion of Christianity with culture. Although in several instances missionaries despaired of the settlers and vowed to go to the tribes, even when they consciously made this choice their methods showed that they had not made a real distinction between Christianity and Western culture. Efforts to learn the language of the people were sporadic and meager. Even today there are

[9] *Ibid.*, p. 208.

missionaries living in stations in the interior who cannot so
much as exchange a greeting with the people in the nearby
village. In almost every case missionaries to the tribes have
begun by establishing schools to teach English and the rudi-
ments of Western civilization. In his missionary journal Melville
B. Cox wrote in 1833, "The great difficulty in instructing the
natives has been to keep them entirely from native influence."[10] Under such a regimen the children of tribal parents
became Westernized and "Christianized" up and out of contact
with their tribal cousins. They became assimilated into the
Americo-Liberian pattern. To a large extent becoming a Christian still carries the stigma of joining a "foreign" tribe. In Loma
villages I have had old men look at me in surprise when I asked
why they had never been baptized, and say, "I never went to
school." The task of providing an education for the children of
the settlers and a few tribal children was a worthy effort; but the
kind of education received effectively insulated Christians from
contact with the tribes and prevented any widespread turning to
Christ among the tribal people.

In all fairness to the Christians and missionaries working
among the settlers, it must be said that there was a tremendous
lot to be done among the "civilized" group on the coast. It is
estimated that only from 14 to 20 per cent of the original
settlers were Christians when they got off the boats. And this
brings us to another reason why Christianity did not spread
from the civilized Liberians to the tribes, which is that, on the
whole, the settlers did not bear very faithful witness to their
Lord. Among them were some outstandingly dedicated men, but
the lives of most colonists spoke louder than a preacher's words.
Life in Liberia was rough. The colonists were frequently under
attack. Sickness was rife; crops failed. The tribesmen cheated
the settlers and the settlers the tribesmen. Disputes could not be
settled peaceably in courts of law, since neither settlers nor
tribesmen fully recognized each others' courts. In their struggle
for survival the settlers gave the tribal people much cause for
stumbling. The natives needed no interpreter to understand
injustice and deceit. Whenever a "Christian" robbed a tribal

[10] *Ibid.*, p. 115.

man of his land, his dignity, or his wife, he gave the lie to the Gospel that was being proclaimed.

In sum, three things kept the tribesmen from becoming Christians. First, the war between the pagan tribes and the settlers kept the former geographically isolated from the Christians. Second, the tribesmen never considered Christianity a real possibility for themselves because it was identified with a foreign culture. Third, unfortunately the moral laxness and social injustice of the settlers in their relations with the tribes did not commend Christianity as a way of life. Today, probably 85 per cent of the citizens of Liberia are non-Christians. There are scores of towns and hundreds of small villages where there is no church. A pattern has been established that has hindered the growth of the Church in the past and continues to limit its expansion today.

However, in this era of rapid social change the circumstances that impeded church growth are rapidly diminishing. In 1920 the interior was brought under the full control of the Liberian Government and opened up to missionaries. This made it possible for several denominations to begin work among the remote tribes. Since World War II, roads have been pushed into the interior, further breaking down tribal isolation. It is easy now for a village man to visit the cities on the coast and see the world for himself; he has been brought into contact with "civilized" men who are not missionaries or even Christians, and has begun to distinguish between Christianity and civilization. While he has been learning that every "civilized" person is not a Christian, some of his fellow villagers have been converted and he has seen examples of faithful Christians who were not "civilized." The seed has been planted. If the Churches are willing to experiment and find new modes of evangelism to break out of the confining patterns and assumptions of the past, the time is ripe for a discipling of the tribes in Liberia.

The story of the growth of the Church in Liberia is the story of the growth of the denominations. The denominational pattern of Protestantism familiar to the colonists and to the missionaries from America was carried over into Liberia, as it was to all mission fields. A knowledge of the struggles the Liberian Churches experienced and the way in which they dealt with them

is indispensable to those in Liberia who must shape a bold new
plan for the future growth of the Church. The insights to be
gained have an application beyond the borders of this African
country. Just as Liberia faced the problems of an independent
nation a century before most of the rest of Africa, so also the
Church in Liberia at least started to grapple with difficult issues
which many African Christians have only recently begun to
face.

> Among these were nationalism, the relation of an educated
> elite, which included some clergy, to the mass of tribal
> people, the call of trained church workers to assume posts in
> government, the search for indigenous expressions of the
> faith once delivered, and an understandable suspicion of
> foreign control and involvement. It is difficult to say that the
> Church in any land ever solves these problems, but at least
> the Liberian Church had begun to face them by 1875.[11]

It is outside the scope of this book to give even a summary of
the history of each denomination. An excellent account of the
Churches in Liberia is given in Walter Cason's doctoral thesis,
"The Growth of the Church in the Liberian Environment."[12]
Unfortunately for churchmen in Liberia, this valuable work has
never been published. In the following pages I have briefly
described the existing work and expansion of the major denominations active in the country, with special attention to instances
of rapid church growth and to the relationships and thinking
which have contributed to the patterns of growth that developed.

THE BAPTIST CHURCHES

Three different streams of Baptist tradition have planted
churches in Liberia. First are the Baptist Churches which stand
in direct historical continuity with the original Baptist settlers
and still preserve some of the traditions of the pre-Civil War
Baptist Churches in the American South out of which they
came. Second are several small independent groups which have
broken off from this main stream of Baptist growth in Liberia,

[11] *Ibid.*, p. 325.
[12] See Bibliography.

or have been geographically isolated from the larger group. These groups have traditions rooted in the Negro Baptist Churches in America from which their founding missionaries came. Third are the churches that have grown out of the more recent endeavors of white missionaries of the Mid-Liberian Baptist Mission and the Liberian Inland Mission.

The first church to be built on Liberian soil was Providence Baptist Church. The congregation was organized on board the *S.S. Elizabeth*, which brought the first settlers. Some of their descendants still worship with the congregation in Monrovia, in the building that was erected in 1827. Providence Baptist Church is the oldest permanent building in Liberia and the oldest Baptist Church in Africa with an uninterrupted history. Almost all the colonists who were Christians were either Baptists or Methodists. This gave those two denominations an advantage for growth over the others. It also meant, however, that they started with the problem of isolation within the Americo-Liberian community which other denominations encountered only after developing a constituency among the civilized group.[13]

The Christian Church known and brought over by the first settlers was the Church of the pre-Civil War American South. At that time, plantation owners and their slaves all worshiped in the same building—though with segregated seating. Only much later, in the 1880's, when the all-Negro Baptist denominations began to emerge in America, did those Churches form their present missionary relations with their Liberian fellows. The traditions of the original settlers have not been completely submerged.

Before the Civil War the Church was the only field in which Negro leadership was free to develop and the people free to express themselves.[14] Slavery had destroyed the Negro family as a social institution. Political and government activities were denied them. In America, therefore, the local church became the dominant social organization for the Negro community. Young men with outstanding ability and leadership potential

[13] Cason, *op. cit.*, p. 164.
[14] *Ibid.*, p. 45.

became pastors, and conversely, when opportunities for political expression and leadership did arise, the ministers were often the only men with the training and leadership experience who could fill the role. It was just such young men who led whole congregations of emigrants to Liberia, and who filled responsible positions of leadership in the life of the new republic. The Church served many more functions for the Negro community than for the dominant whites, including involvement in politics. This pattern was carried over into the churches in Liberia, where the Church has tended to interpret its role in society rather broadly.

The Negro Churches in America influenced the Churches in Liberia through the missionaries and emigrant preachers who went there. This influence was stronger in Baptist Churches than in any other denomination, because of their connection with the entirely Negro Baptist denominations in America—most notably the National Baptist Convention and the Lott Carey Missionary Society. The missionaries sent by other denominations were predominantly white (for example, no Negro Methodist missionaries were sent to Liberia between 1936 and 1948). The Negro missionaries often lacked the academic training of their white counterparts in other denominations, but their race and experience of discrimination gave them added zeal to improve the condition of the Africans. In America, Liberia was often viewed as an experiment which would prove the racial equality of the Negro. In 1923 a Baptist board secretary appealed for recruits for Liberia among American Negroes by saying, "Who knows but that through Liberia, the Negro is to come into his own."[15] Many Negro missionaries who came to Liberia in the twenties and thirties of this century were strongly influenced by the thinking of the Garvey movement among American Negroes, which advocated a return to Africa and the improvement of social conditions there. These missionaries were eager to improve the situation of "their people," but expended little effort in evangelization or church planting. The names of some of the Baptist institutions founded during this period are

[15] *Ibid.*, p. 321.

indicative of the trend: Suehn *Industrial* Mission, Bendu *Industrial* Mission, Bible *Industrial* Academy.

Whereas missionaries of other denominations made frequent trips home which kept them in contact with current developments, the most influential Baptists were emigrant preachers or missionaries who spent long terms on the field without a break. Thus, for example, the wave of evangelical revival that swept the Negro Churches in America in the 1930's almost completely bypassed the Baptists in Liberia. Other denominations in Liberia had annual meetings which brought them together to discuss mutual problems and make overall plans. The Baptists, until recently, had none.

One real advantage the Negro missionaries had over their white counterparts was that there was no racial barrier, and they often lived right with the people. Several, even in recent times, have given up their American citizenship and become Liberian citizens, their children marrying into the Liberian community. These missionaries accepted the Americo-Liberian society and the place of the Church in that society rather less critically than the white missionaries of other denominations, and this may be one reason why the Baptist Church today is almost completely contained within the English-speaking communities of the coast—a containment which, more than any other factor, has limited its expansion in Liberia.

Another factor that hindered Baptist expansion was the relative poverty of the Negro community in America, which made it impossible for their churches to send sufficient funds for expansion to the interior. During the Civil War, when all funds from America were cut off, and in times of economic depression, the progress of all the denominations suffered. But even in prosperity and peace, the Baptists in Liberia were forced to rely on their own resources for the life of their congregations. In 1855, for example, they received only $4,000 in subsidy as compared to the $24,000 received by the Methodists. From the first, the Baptists made attempts at self-support. In 1875 Providence Baptist Church in Monrovia assessed each adult male member 12½¢ per month. A system of dues prevails in many Liberian Baptist Churches today. In 1951 the Liberian Baptist Convention had a total budget of $42,000, of which only $7,600 was contributed from abroad. (Though the superintendent of the National Baptist Mission spent more than $100,000 in that year on schools and hospitals, and the Lott Carey Mission another $40,000.) This relative lack of foreign support has helped to make the Baptists the most indigenous denomination in Liberia, but has also kept them from expanding to the interior.

Missionary work among the tribes of the interior, which involves transportation, support personnel, and eleemosynary work (stipulated by the Constitution of the republic), is considerably more expensive than church work in the settlement. In 1923, for example, when the Lutheran mission was opened at Zorzor near the Guinea border, all goods and supplies had to be carried by porters from Monrovia, 175 miles away—a five-day trip. The mission paid $3.36 to the chief for each porter. In 1931 cement for building cost six times its Monrovia price just to transport it to Zorzor; salt cost three times its Monrovia price.[16] The lack of large subsidies led the Baptists to conduct the least expensive type of missionary endeavor, near the coast. The many Baptist pastors who preached on Sunday but earned their living at other work were largely confined to the Americo-Liberian community, where opportunity for employment existed. Another result of this lack of mission support is that the Baptists have relatively fewer institutions in Liberia than the other major denominations. In recent years, however, as the Negro Church in America has become more affluent, correspondingly more money has been available. In 1955 a program was begun to upgrade existing Baptist institutions and establish new ones.[17]

The Baptists in Liberia have also suffered from interdenominational rivalries which hindered the growth of the Church. The corresponding secretary of the National Baptist Convention, U.S.A., wrote in 1923, "In the Republic of Liberia there are three sets of missionaries representing the Negro Baptists of this country. By virtue of their home ties, they are essentially enemies in Africa. This is serious, injurious and unjustifiable."[18]

[16] Whetstone, *Lutheran Mission in Liberia,* p. 81.

[17] Cason, *op. cit.,* p. 401.

[18] *Ibid.,* p. 329.

But whatever the situation in the past, much has been done in recent years to consolidate the work of the various groups and increase cooperation among them.

The Liberian Baptist Missionary and Educational Convention is the main organ for cooperation. About half the estimated 14,000 Baptists in Liberia are now associated with this convention.[19] This group has relations with several mission boards in America, but the leadership is in the hands of Liberian churchmen.[20] Dr. William Richard Tolbert, Jr., Vice President of the republic, is president of the Convention. Mr. Tolbert is also World President of the Baptist World Alliance. The contacts he has made with the leaders of Baptist Churches in America in this latter capacity have brought both missionaries and increased contributions to the Baptist Churches in Liberia.

The National Baptist Convention, U.S.A., Inc. now operates the Klay mission founded by Dr. H. S. Jones and the Suehn Industrial Academy. They have built the Carrie V. Dyer Memorial Hospital in Monrovia. This hospital and nurses' home were completed under the direction of John B. Falconer, mission superintendent for West Africa of the National Baptist Convention, Inc. In 1963 it had a budget of $194,556, making it the largest Baptist institution in Liberia.[21] The Liberian Government purchased the hospital in 1963, and Dr. Falconer is administrator. The National Baptist Convention, U. S. A. (unincorporated), has sent missionaries and made contributions to a mission in Sinoe County. The major work of the Lott Carey Baptist mission is their high school at Brewerville. They also operate a rubber farm at Bamboota and a small evangelistic enterprise at Salala.

In 1960, in response to appeals by Augustus Marwieh, a Liberian student who studied at the Golden Gate Baptist Seminary in California, and by several Americans who had worked in Liberia, the Southern Baptists re-entered the country after being absent since 1875. Southern Baptist mission board executives had met Dr. Tolbert at the Baptist World Congress in

[19] *Ibid.,* p. 401.
[20] *Ibid.,* p. 402.
[21] *Ibid.,* p. 403.

1960. They were favorably impressed on subsequent visits to the field. The Southern Baptists are contributing both men and money to strengthen Ricks Institute and develop a theology department there. They are making plans to continue the work of several independent Baptist missionaries and are encouraging the cooperation between various Baptist groups in Liberia.

The churches in the Liberian Baptist Missionary and Educational Convention limit their work almost entirely to the civilized community. Their outreach to the tribal people consists mostly of weekend visits by students to a few outstations near the schools at Suehn, Ricks, and Brewerville.

In the immediate future there will almost surely be a further expansion of Baptist enterprises. If the Baptists are to play their part in evangelizing the tribal peoples of Liberia, they should expand their institutions among them, with a corresponding expansion of evangelism in the villages. This will not happen automatically; it will require a bold new plan, a conscious decision to follow the plan, and concentrated effort to carry it out.

The Independents and Southern Baptists. Individual congregations of the Baptist Church are almost completely autonomous. This congregational type of church polity suits many aspects of the situation in the civilized sections of Liberia and has been a favorable factor in the expansion of the Baptist Church there. Under it a local congregation may ordain a minister. This has meant that Baptist congregations, even when separated by schism or geographical isolation, have been able to carry on a full ministry of word and sacrament without highly trained ministers, in several cases independent of any missionary subsidy from abroad.

Three outstanding examples of such missions deserve special mention. First, the Klay Institute, an independent mission station directed for more than forty years by H. S. Jones, a Negro minister-physician from Mississippi. His work has been incorporated into the work of the National Baptists since 1950. More recently this mission has been notable for its efforts at local support through agricultural projects.[22] Second is the

22 *Ibid.,* p. 104

mission of Mother George in and around Greenville in Sinoe County. In 1961, at the age of 85, Mother George turned her work over to the Southern Baptists. She had thirteen churches. Her faithful witness over the years had prepared the tribal people in surrounding villages to become Christian, so that within two and a half years the Southern Baptist missionaries were able to organize churches in thirteen other villages. They also operate nine small elementary schools in villages where there are no public schools. Mother George had no formal theological training herself and gave none to the preachers she supervised. Especially in her later years, church discipline declined and administration faltered. Among her workers were some "salary" Christians and some with low moral standards. But the fact remains that churches were planted—churches in which revival and renewal are now taking place. One of her most important achievements was the training of several young men, among them Augustus Marwieh, who after further education in America is making an outstanding contribution to the work of the Baptist Church in Liberia.[23]

Third is the independent mission of Dr. and Mrs. Horton. They came to Liberia in 1917 as missionaries of the National Baptist Convention. After spending the first term in Grand Bassa, Dr. Horton became superintendent of the work in Monrovia. A chance meeting with one of his former Bassa members led him to "Bassatown on the beach." There, in a swampy area near the spot where the Firestone garage is today, were three little huts and a few garden-sized rice farms. Mrs. Horton remembers the beginnings of that work.

> They slept all day and gambled all night. We found one man who wanted to talk God-palaver. We talked and sang. The people asked us to come back. That's how we started, with the people on the beach. They put up a mud hut with a thatched roof for their church. We had some wonderful revivals there in 1922, and in 1923 founded St. Simon's Baptist Church.[24]

[23] From an interview with the Rev. John H. Carpenter, May 1964.
[24] From an interview with Mrs. Daniel W. Horton, May 1964.

Dr. Horton's work among the Bassa included the founding of the Bassa Brotherhood and Protective Society, which provided members who paid a shilling a month with burial benefits of between $75 and $100. It also included the acquisition of land for a Christian community surrounding a centrally located school. A misunderstanding over the purchase of the land led the mission board in America to withdraw support from the Hortons. Without financial aid from abroad they nevertheless elected to remain in Liberia and became citizens of the republic. With their leadership, after a few years of struggling, St. Simon's began to grow.

Some of the Bassa members working at the Firestone plantation held worship services at the camp. They came to Dr. Horton and said, "Pa, we've started a church at Section 14, and we need you to come and baptize." In this way several congregations were started, which in 1938 Dr. Horton organized into a conference. There are now thirty-six churches in the conference, three in Monrovia alone. The conference has three ordained men who supervise the work of the congregations. Every church has a leader who preaches and holds services, and calls the ordained men for weddings and to give the sacraments. Revivals are held in the churches twice a year. Mrs. Horton is the supervising principal at the Bassa Community School, which has grown out of their work to its present size of a total enrollment of 1200.[25]

In 1944 a representative of the Southern Baptist missionary board, stranded in Monrovia between planes, talked with Dr. Horton about the possibility of the Southern Baptists continuing his work after his retirement. Twenty years later machinery for such a continuation was set up.

Describing the means of self-support in the group of churches started by Mother George, the supervising Southern Baptist missionary Rev. John M. Carpenter told me that, while anxious to strengthen the congregations, "we do not intend to make them dependent on our mission. If it should become necessary for mission support to be cut off tomorrow, they would be able to stand on their own feet." Presumably the self-reliance of con-

[25] *Ibid.*

gregations associated with Dr. Horton's conference will be preserved in the same way.

Baptist Mid-Missions. A totally different stream of Baptist tradition came to Liberia in 1931 with the arrival of Rev. and Mrs. Gordon Mellick of the Canadian Regular Baptists.[26] If the older Baptist missionary societies were uncritical in their acceptance of the Americo-Liberian Church, it may be said that the reaction of these Baptists was just the opposite. They completely bypassed the civilized Liberians and carried the Gospel strictly to the tribes. There were nine missionaries working at two stations in the Bassa tribe—New Cess and Zondo—before financial difficulties arising from the depression forced the home board to abandon this new field.

The missionaries, however, returned to work in Liberia, some with the Mid-Liberian Baptist Mission, some with the Worldwide Evangelism Crusade, which in Liberia is called the Liberian Inland Mission. Evangelists of the latter mission carried the Gospel to Tapeta in 1937. Since then they have reopened the original stations in the Bassa tribe and expanded the work. The mission also has two stations in the Mano tribe, including Sanikwelli, and two among the Gio tribe. In 1950 evangelistic services were begun at the Firestone plantation. The Liberian Inland Mission operates six clinics staffed by missionary nurses, and schools at all its main stations.[27] The 1962 *World Christian Handbook* reports 44 missionaries, including wives, for this mission.[28]

The Mid-Liberian Baptist Mission has stations in the Gio, Mano, Bassa, Kran, and Kpelle tribes. The largest concentration of missionaries is the 13 who work at Tapeta. The *World Christian Handbook* for 1957 reported 88 preaching points but only 129 communicants for this mission.[29] In 1964 they reported only 250 communing members. They operated five schools with a total enrollment of nearly 300, a leprosarium,

[26] Cason, *op. cit.,* p. 331.
[27] From an interview with Rev. J. T. Lyons, May 1964.
[28] Grubb, ed., *World Christian Handbook, 1962,* p. 72.
[29] *Ibid.,* p. 72.

and a clinic at Yille and another at Tapeta.[30] Both of these missions emphasize preaching the Gospel to the rural areas. The following are examples of how this is carried out: (a) The Bible Institute at Tapeta offers a three-year program for evangelists who have had some elementary schooling. This institute is providing trained leadership for the churches of the area. (b) The production of Christian literature moves forward among the Bassa, Mano, and Gio. Full-time linguists have been assigned to the Bassa and Mano areas. The Wycliffe linguists' course is recommended for all evangelistic missionaries before coming to this field. This is the only mission in Liberia that operates a press. (c) A small airplane carries Bible students or missionaries into isolated villages for weekend preaching or evangelistic campaigns. Seventeen airstrips have been cut in the forest near these villages. The location of the recently opened Keaple Station was determined after a survey of the area from the air.[31]

The missionaries recognize that educational and medical work are helpful but testify that "the basic and most significant change to be made and the greatest service to be rendered are in the relation to Jesus Christ. Those who have accepted Him are then more interested in adopting new habits of hygiene and learning a new technique in agriculture and other fields." This commendable emphasis on soul-winning should theoretically result in the rapid expansion of the Church, and there have been a few breakthroughs. A series of revivals in the Gio tribe, for example, resulted in more than seventy conversions. But the membership figures reported indicate that this growth has not been sustained, nor is it typical.

Though it is the policy of these missions to emphasize evangelism, in actual practice they are heavily institutionalized. When the daily efforts of all the missionaries are tabulated and expenditures for all causes examined, it is apparent that these missions spend as large a proportion of their time and money on medical and educational work as do the other denominations in Liberia. Their schools and clinics have an advantage, however,

[30] Response to a questionnaire received in November 1964.
[31] Cason, op. cit., p. 446.

over the huge institutions of some other denominations in that they are less elaborate. They could probably be taken over and operated by the emerging indigenous Church if American support were cut off. On the other hand, the number of Christians in each local congregation and the number of converts per missionary year of service is also correspondingly smaller.

The missionaries blame polygamy for this lack of growth. The tribal culture accepts it, while these missions take a very strict stand against baptizing the members of polygamous households. Enforcement of these rules has not only limited the accessions to the Church, but has meant a continued loss in membership through excommunication. Two missionaries interviewed listed polygamy as the major hindrance to evangelization of the tribes.[32]

A high standard of personal holiness in the church can serve as a booster to evangelism, if the standards are met and enforced by the Christian community itself. To the extent, however, that they represent the reaction of foreign missionaries to the culture of the people, they become unnecessary stumbling blocks to acceptance of the Gospel. One missionary told me, "Our people need to understand the life of faith in Christ without having to have a law to make them do something."[33] I would agree with this and add only that missionaries, too, need a faith—a faith to trust that if they bring a man to Christ, the Spirit of Christ in him will teach him how to live his life in Christ without, as this missionary said, "a law to make him do something." Here again the congregational autonomy of the Baptist Church policy has somewhat alleviated the situation. Local congregations are taking over the enforcement of church discipline. The mission polity is to let the local church council decide who should be baptized and to "keep hands off" once they have organized a church.

It is regrettable that there is little organizational or geographical contact between the Mid-Missions group and other Baptist

[32] From an interview with Mr. Percy Clubine and Rev. Tom Jackson, June 1964.
[33] Lyons interview.

mission organizations in Liberia.[34] This separation from other denominations is such a firm tenet of the sponsoring bodies in America that it seems doubtful whether missionaries of the Mid-Missions and Liberian Inland Mission could establish official relations with other Baptists. However, even unofficial fellowship would be very rewarding for both sides. The Baptists on the coast need the experience and insights Mid-Missions has gained in carrying the Gospel to the tribes. Mid-Missions for its own part needs to learn how to adapt its theology to meet the challenges of the Americo-Liberian culture, which is already pressing in on the villages where its missionaries work and is surely the wave of the future. It may be that circumstances will make it impossible for these missionaries to get together, in which case such encounters will doubtless be carried out by the generation of Liberian Baptists who are now only school children.

THE METHODIST CHURCH

The Methodist Church in Liberia is the largest denomination in the republic. This is without counting the membership of two sister communions, the African Methodist Episcopal Zion and the African Methodist Episcopal Church of the U.S.A., both of which have small missions in Liberia. The Methodist Church, which is affiliated with the Methodist Church in the United States, had 17,364 full members on the active roll in 1964.[35] Since the membership rolls were trimmed in 1960, these figures are among the most dependable reported by any Church in the republic. Indeed, if the total number of people in Liberia who call themselves Methodist were counted, it would be at least twice as large. This is one denomination in which scattered growth has taken place. But these instances of good growth are not commensurate with the outstanding opportunities for growth that existed, and they fall still farther short of what can and should be realized in the future. This is especially striking when one looks at the total monies from foreign mission boards

[34] Cason, *op. cit.*, p. 405.
[35] Methodist Church, "Statistics of the 114th Session of the Liberian Annual Conference," January 22-26, 1964. Mimeographed.

(and in recent years, government subsidies) which the Methodist Church in Liberia has received.

"For a quarter of a century Liberia was the only foreign outpost of the Methodist Church in America, for half a century its only mission on the continent of Africa."[36] From its infancy this Church was kept going by substantial mission subsidy. For most of the time since the nation gained independence, and even before, the Methodist mission has been financially more solvent than the government. In the 1830's, for example, the Methodist Missionary Society "printed tickets of various valuations which could be used as offering since there was no circulating medium. When the colonizing society had no money and the mission still had reserves, traders along the coast would accept the mission tickets at face value but not those of the society."[37] But more important than the money spent is the faithful, dedicated service of men and women, Americans and Liberians, who have served this Church. Today the Methodist Church influences the life of the whole nation, primarily through the labors of outstanding lay leaders, including President William V. S. Tubman.

In the Methodist Church in Liberia there are three distinct types of church or mission approach. The first is the Methodist Church in the Americo-Liberian communities in Monrovia and the settlements. The second type is represented by the Church on the Kru coast, where whole families and even whole villages of Kru tribesmen have in the past accepted Christianity in people movement fashion. The movement has stopped, but the Church remains. Third is the mission to the interior tribes. The missionary stations at Ganta in the Mano tribe and at Gbarnga in the Kpelle tribe are good examples of this approach. So far, very little church planting has taken place in the last-mentioned missions. The fact that these three distinct approaches to the mission of the Church, and the corresponding differences in the pattern of church growth, all exist within the same denomina-

[36] Ivan Lee Holt, *The Methodists of the World* (New York: Methodist Board of Missions and Church Extension, 1950), p. 76.

[37] Cason, *op. cit.*, p. 125.

tion should put the Methodist Church in a unique position to
judge which experiment has best realized the potential for rapid
church growth, and to use that method in its advance to the
tribes in the future.

Several factors inhibiting growth can be well illustrated by
the problem facing the Methodists in the English-speaking communities. To a man, the church leaders I interviewed were
concerned with developing an adequate ministry for their congregations. This problem is an old one. As early as 1834 the
Rev. Rufus Spaulding noted that the growth of the Church
must be through African pastors, not only because white missionaries seemed unable to stand the climate, but "more especially because it has been God's usual method in carrying on
His work to raise up instruments from among His own people."[38]

The Methodist Church needs to develop full-time, well-
trained, adequately paid pastors. So many problems of the
Church are related to this matter that to broach the subject is
like opening Pandora's box. In Liberia some have left the
ministry to serve the Republic in government positions—or, as
often happened, have tried to do both jobs at once. Others who
felt called to preach had to supplement their income by farming
or other work, because their congregations were unable to pay a
living wage from the offerings.[39] The result in both cases was
that the Church had the ministry of only a part-time pastor.

In 1848 the Methodist mission board expressed the desir-
ability of a full-time ministry. "We hope now that the Rubicon
is passed, and Liberia has become independent, there will be
less occasion for them [the pastors] to leave the Word of God
to serve tables or republics."[40] Though the problem has long
been recognized, the situation remains in a large number of congregations today. The ministers I interviewed who serve congregations in these circumstances are the first to recognize the handicaps of a part-time ministry. I found them to be dedicated men.
They have to do supplementary work because the congrega-

[38] *Ibid.*, p. 118.
[39] *Ibid.*, p. 129.
[40] *Ibid.*, p. 201 (Quoting the Twenty-ninth Annual Report).

tions, tied by patterns of the past, think they cannot afford to pay a full-time pastor. Actually, in the new era of economic expansion in Liberia, many of them would now be quite able. As the economy grows, this will be true for more and more churches.

The congregations have come to accept the idea of the minister as a part-time man. They do not know the advantages of having a full-time ministry. In some of these congregations, groups of laymen, deacons, and elders do a great deal of visiting the sick and shut-in, and counseling. If such congregations do get full-time pastors, it is hoped that the laymen will continue in their service and not leave everything to the pastor as a paid professional, as is the case in so many congregations in the United States.[41]

The problem of the part-time pastor is that the relationship of mutual responsibility which should exist between pastor and people has been undermined, if not entirely destroyed. The pastor is tempted to put his energy into his paying job and make few sacrifices for his congregation. The people, for their part, do not feel a responsibility to contribute to his support. This has an effect on their whole stewardship pattern. Here the old saying applies: "You get only what you pay for."

The Churches in Liberia have begun to discuss and even strive for self-support. But the established stewardship pattern and the habits formed during years of dependence upon mission subsidy from abroad are hard to overcome. Attempts at self-support take the form of money-raising campaigns rather than a stress on sacrificial giving. "Very few churches make a budget and seek pledges for regular giving to it from their members, though many charge dues which must be paid before the member may receive the services of the church, such as marriage or burial."[42]

The Churches have turned to "rallies" as a recognized means of raising money for self-support.

[41] From an interview with the Rev. T. T. Roberts, Monrovia, June 1964.
[42] Cason, *op. cit.*, p. 414.

In many local rallies more effort is made to obtain gifts from officials and merchants in Monrovia than to inspire the members of the congregation concerned to practice steward-ship. At the time of the rally itself a leading official "lifts" the collection and by his own contribution and those which he is able to stimulate others to provide a significant sum may be realized.[43]

The hinterland rallies of the late fifties obtained annual sums of $50,000 for the Methodist local board of missions projects. Actual figures were:

1957	$45,184.40
1958	118,515.91
1959	141,366.43
1960	204,723.60
*1961	50,000.00
1962	50,000.00
1963	50,000.00
1964	50,000.00

The first advance rally in 1957 produced over $50,000 for projects of the Methodist Church, and subsequent rallies have brought such increase that now over $200,000 may be col-lected in one year. This is the first time the Liberian Metho-dists have made a larger contribution to their Church than that of the American mission board. . . . In recent years the Baptists, Presbyterians, Episcopalians, and Roman Catholics have held similar rallies. The Episcopalians, at least, have raised amounts similar to those of the Methodists by their efforts. These modern programs consist of a series of rallies in the port cities, each being led by a prominent official and soliciting contributions from the foreign merchants and citi-zens of all denominations in the area. Some effort is also made to obtain funds from the interior tribes along the major road. The appeal is made specifically that of reaching a certain financial goal. There is seldom any reference to the use to be made of the offering, though the obviously benefi-

[43] *Ibid.*
  * After 1960 only $50,000 of the total monies collected was set aside for hinterland expansion.

cial application of previous rallies has certainly stimulated giving. The major stimulus for giving, however, is the prestige and power of the one conducting the rally.[44]

This last sentence especially indicates that "self-support" gained through rallies, rather than restoring the interdependence of pastor and people, is likely to cause them to depend more and more upon the prestige of government officials.

The Methodist Church has a plan for training pastors on several levels. A full-time worker was assigned in 1956 to travel throughout Liberia offering refresher courses to the pastors and training for evangelists. Second, there is a Bible school at Gbarnga which trains men who have grade-school education to serve in village churches. Third, for more highly trained men the Methodist Church cooperates with the Episcopalians at Cuttington College and Divinity School. The plan is a good one, but the number of men who have come forward to be trained as ordained pastors has been disappointing.[45]

Another factor affecting the growth of the Church is the strong emphasis on mission schools and education. The feeling that "Liberia's redemption cannot be solved apart from education," has led to this mission policy.[46] The Methodist school system is second to that of no other Church or mission in the republic. The problems for church growth posed by institutions will be discussed in Chapter V; suffice it to mention here only how it aggravates the problem of self-support. For the Liberian Church to assume the financial support of its ministers and construct its own church buildings is one thing, but to take over the burden of a large school system is quite another matter. Mission money from American and government subsidy is used at present to operate the Methodist schools, and government and mission subsidies will be necessary for the foreseeable future to keep mission schools open. The government may take over completely the support and operation of certain schools, as in the case of the Booker T. Washington Institute at Kakata

[44] *Ibid.*, p. 415.
[45] From an interview with the Rev. B. B. Coefield, Monrovia, June 1964.
[46] Cason, *loc. cit.*

in 1953. The Methodist Church operates a high school in Monrovia, called the College of West Africa, as well as numerous grade schools, Monrovia College, and a high school at Cape Palmas.

Self-government is potentially an important factor in the growth of the Church. Ever since Liberia gained its independence, it has been a bone of contention among Methodists that they could choose the President who governed their nation, but had no voice in the choice of a bishop for their Church. In fact, they had no residing bishop. Early efforts to form an independent Church in the late 1880's failed for lack of sufficient support. After Methodist unification in the United States in 1939, the Methodist Church in Liberia was administered by the Methodist Church in America as part of the African Central Conference, which included mission work in Angola, the Belgian Congo, Mozambique, and the Rhodesias. This link with colonial Africa, though it seemed like good strategy to officials in America, was very unpopular in Liberia. In 1944 a new plan was put into effect by which a Bishop of Liberia would be elected by the Central Jurisdiction in America. Willis J. King, an American, the president of Gammon Seminary, was chosen. He was unable to spend much time in Liberia, especially during the last three years of his administration, since he was also responsible for three conferences in America. Bishop Price A. Taylor has guided the Church since 1956.[47] The issue of having their own bishop was underlined in 1959 when the General Conference of the African Methodist Episcopal Zion Church in America elected a Liberian pastor, the Rev. S. Dorn Lartey, bishop at the suggestion of the Liberian Conference of the Church.

Under the existing Methodist system Liberia, with only one conference, had too few ordained ministers to elect its own bishop. However, in 1964 the General Conference in America adopted a plan presented by Bishop Taylor which makes it possible for Liberia and certain other countries to affiliate with the Conference and elect their own bishops. In 1965 the Liberian Annual Conference voted to follow this new course of action

[47] *Ibid.*, p. 409.

and became an affiliate of the General Conference in America.[48] Early in 1966 the Liberian conference convened in special session and elected Stephen Trowen Nagbe—the first citizen of Liberia to become a Methodist bishop.

The Kru Coast. The Methodist Church on the Kru coast faces an entirely different situation, which holds exciting possibilities for church growth. Here the Methodist mission made early efforts to take the Gospel to the tribes. In 1834 John Hersey, a local preacher and assistant agent of the Maryland State Colonization Society, advised the board to "abandon Monrovia for work in the interior and to instruct missionaries to use local food and housing, to accommodate their living to the customs and usages of the natives."[49] Several attempts were made. In 1844 two missionaries went to the Gola tribe. Three stations were operating among the Grebo near Cape Palmas as early as 1845. The difficulties of reaching the tribes mentioned in the introduction to this chapter effectively hindered these early Methodist efforts. In the late 1880's, however, some stations were established on the Kru coast. In 1909 that mission was strengthened by the coming of Walter B. Williams, a missionary who had had previous experience in Angola. The Church flourished. In the preceding ten years, from 1900 to 1910, the membership of the Sinoe district, which includes the Kru coast, increased by a mere 99 members from 267 to 366 for an average growth of only 3½ per cent a year. Nine years later, in 1919, the Sinoe district reported a membership of 1,248—an average increase of 27 per cent per year.[50]

The Sinoe district actually accounted for more than half the growth of the whole Methodist Church in Liberia for that period. Monrovia and Cape Palmas between them accounted for most of the rest, but both these districts, as "civilized" centers, were gaining immigrant populations. Sinoe was not. The membership gains there represented converts among pagan

[48] From an interview with M. Caldwell, Eugene, Ore., April 1965.
[49] Cason, *op. cit.*, p. 119.
[50] Methodist Church, "Statistics No. 1," *Minutes, Liberia Annual Conference,* January 31 to February 7, 1900; "Statistics No. 1," *Minutes, Liberia Annual Conference,* March 2-7, 1910; "Statistician's Report, Conference for 1919," *Minutes, Liberia Annual Conference,* 1919.

tribesmen. Their resistance to the Gospel had broken down and changed to an attitude of acceptance. Unfortunately the rapid movement of the Kru people into the Church stopped as abruptly as it had begun. Recent figures show that the Methodists on the Kru coast have lost the momentum of growth. It is interesting to note, however, that the momentum of expansion has not stopped but has merely passed on to other denominations.[51] This has happened largely by default. For years Methodist missionaries leaving the district were not replaced; today there is not a single Methodist missionary in the whole area. Well-trained administrative personnel have not been available at the top level. Until recently even the district superintendent had only a grade-school education.[52]

When one visits Methodist congregations on the Kru coast today, one recognizes that although these churches are not growing, they are very much the "people's" church. The congregations are not large in membership, but members attend worship regularly and carry on the life of the church on their own. These are not Americo-Liberian congregations of educated English-speaking members. The members live in tribal villages. The services are in the Kru language.

One of the two Methodists to graduate from Cuttington Divinity School in recent years is David Doe, who came from the Kru coast. After teaching at Ganta and serving as pastor of the First Methodist Church of Monrovia, this outstanding young man has been appointed to a district back on the Kru coast. With this kind of leadership, it may be that Methodists there will be on the march once again.[53]

The Mission to the Tribes. A third Methodist approach to evangelism was made at Ganta in 1926, when the physician, Dr. George Harley, began his work there in the Mano tribe. For twenty-one years little effort was made to found a church.

[51] Other denominations include Roman Catholic, Episcopal, Pentecostal. From an interview with the Rev. David S. Doe, Monrovia, May 1962. See also Coefield and Caldwell interviews.
[52] Coefield interview.
[53] Caldwell interview.

Not until 1947 was a missionary assigned to full-time evangelistic work.[54] This is perhaps a classic example of the mission station approach to the exclusion of preaching the Gospel and establishing churches. The Ganta station has a large hospital and nurses' training program, a school, a hostel, a church, a sawmill and furniture shop, and a garage.

But in spite of this tremendous investment and expenditure in institutions, there has been almost no growth of the Church. Scattered in four pastoral charges in this district are 203 Christians. These include the Christian students enrolled in the Ganta School. There is some indication that in the villages away from the main station, the Mano people may be ready to respond to the Gospel, perhaps even as the Kru did half a century ago.[55] Efforts in the Bing clan have been especially fruitful, but several factors have limited growth. In the villages where Mano tribesmen are responding favorably to the Gospel, not many can afford to send their children to the mission school. The "civilized" element who do send their children to school are for the most part already members of churches. In the highly institutionalized compound it seems natural for the missionaries to spend a great deal of time in administration and maintenance. They feel they cannot get out to the villages, where the growth potential is high. Another factor is that language study is still not required for missionaries, although it has long been recognized that inability to speak the tribal language is a definite and obvious handicap to church growth. Missionaries who do not know the language spend a disproportionately large amount of their time with school children and others who speak English, rather than with the adult villagers among whom church growth is possible.

These different types of churches are all a part of the Methodist Church in Liberia, a significant example of that unity in the face of diversity which is the unification policy at work. The Church was already established in Liberia before the mission came. The mission, which came to aid the young Church, later

[54] Coefield interview.
[55] Caldwell interview.

established work in places like Ganta and the Kru coast where the young Church had no work.[56] If a people movement among the tribes takes place, the Methodists are in a strategic position to do their share in discipling the nation to Christ.

[56] Coefield interview.

CHAPTER IV

GROWTH OF THE EPISCOPAL, LUTHERAN, AND OTHER CHURCHES

THE EPISCOPAL CHURCH

The Episcopal Church in Liberia is a small but fairly sound ship. It recorded a total baptized membership of 9,043 in 1962, and statistical reports indicate that it has sustained a growth of just under 10 per cent a year for more than fifteen years. For the Americo-Liberian communities, already largely Christian, this is adequate. But, as mentioned earlier, field totals often conceal outstanding local expansion or loss.

The current pattern for church growth in the Episcopal Church is tied closely to the school system, which includes some of the best schools in the republic. There are forty-one elementary schools, three high schools, and Cuttington College.[1] This college was moved from Cape Palmas in 1948 and is now located near Suokoko in the interior, about 130 miles east of Monrovia. The college offers four-year programs in agriculture, education, and arts and sciences, and since the Lutherans completed the Phoebe Hospital at Suokoko in 1965 a B.S. course in nurses' training has been added. The divinity school, located on the same campus, has graduated ten Episcopal priests and several Methodist ministers since it was founded. Thus the Episcopal Church is making a concerted effort to train the leaders of the civilized community of tomorrow.[2] Yet in taking this approach there is always the danger of developing a Church that is educated up and out of touch with the tribal masses. Rapid growth will not take place unless conscious effort is made to avoid this hazard and maintain contact with the tribes.

Beginnings Among the Grebo. Evidently there were not enough Episcopalians aboard the *S.S. Elizabeth* in 1820 to form

[1] Henry B. Cole, *Liberian Yearbook, 1962,* p. 145.
[2] From an interview with the Rev. Burgess Carr, June 1964.

a congregation, so they organized a missionary society instead. In the years that followed, not many of the colonists who arrived from America were Episcopalians. In fact, most had never even heard of that Church before coming to Liberia.

The work of the earliest Episcopal missionaries was centered in Cape Palmas. They concentrated on reaching out to the Grebo tribe in that area, and the earliest rapid church growth that took place in Liberia was the Episcopalian expansion among the Grebo. Some of the missionaries took language study seriously enough so that by 1839 someone had produced a Grebo dictionary, and by 1843 the complete Gospels of Matthew and Mark.[3] At first the response was slow. After ten years of Episcopal missionary work there were only thirty-seven converts, twenty-one of whom were in good standing.[4] Unlike so many of the early attempts to convert the tribes, however, the Episcopalians' effort was continuous, took root, and grew. Surely one of the major factors in this development of the Grebo Church was the continuity of leadership provided in the person of Rev. John Payne. He could speak the Grebo language and translated parts of the Scripture into it. He had an intimate and effective knowledge of Grebo customs, so that in 1842, for example, when he preached a sermon against fetishes, fifteen men in a single village burned their fetishes. In 1851 he was consecrated bishop of Cape Palmas and parts adjacent, and he guided the Church for the next twenty years until his death. Here was a man who was concerned enough to identify with the people and learn their language. He served long enough for the growth he started to mature. In every instance of rapid church expansion among the tribal people in Liberia, one of the contributing factors has been a dedicated missionary or Liberian pastor, such as John Payne.[5]

The Episcopal Church among the Grebo was blessed with two such men. The second was Bishop Samuel David Ferguson.

[3] Cason, "Growth of the Church in the Liberian Environment," p. 149.

[4] *Ibid.*, p. 15.

[5] Varian H. Cassat, *Liberian Palaver* (New York: National Council of Churches, 1952), p. 26.

Born in South Carolina, he had emigrated to Liberia with his family in 1848, and John Payne had helped them to settle near Cape Palmas.[6] Ferguson grew up, received his training, and was ordained in a growing Church among the tribal Grebo. This growth among the tribal people was unique for that time in Liberian history. When he was consecrated bishop in 1885—the first Negro bishop of the Episcopal Church—he was well prepared to continue the growth of the Church among that tribe. An expansion took place in the first ten years of his episcopacy. This was small in comparison with the growth of the Churches in the Gold Coast at the time, but was the only such expansion in Liberia. In 1885 there had been 419 communicants and 30 preaching points. Ten years later there were 1,237 communicants in 63 preaching places in Liberia—not including 35 centers of work across the Cavala River which had meanwhile been lost to the French.[7]

The Episcopal Church was concentrated in the Grebo tribe. This caused the President of Liberia and some others to blame that Church for the Grebo rebellions of 1875, 1893, and 1910. Indeed, all the better-educated Grebo who took part in the revolt had been trained in Episcopal schools. Ferguson vehemently denied any complicity on the part of the Church in this matter. While he had often championed the cause of the natives, he made it clear by quick discipline of a priest and four teachers who had been involved that "the Church would not countenance rebellion and disloyalty."[8]

During this time the Church grew in more than numbers. Ferguson had a genius for drawing young men into the ministry, and he saw the connection between the expansion of the Church and the need for well-trained priests. One of his outstanding achievements was the establishment of Cuttington College at Cape Palmas and the training of a number of capable preachers and spiritual pastors. In the 1920's and early 1930's the mission emphasis shifted to Cape Mount and Bolahun, and the Grebo work was left largely on its own resources, "which

[6] *Ibid.,* p. 30.
[7] Cason, *op. cit.,* p. 721.
[8] *Ibid.,* p. 275.

proved insufficient for maintaining the large boarding schools."[9] The leadership training program lapsed, so that there were fewer trained pastors in 1944 than there had been in 1916, when Bishop Ferguson died.[10] Today almost every congregation in the Cape Palmas subdistrict is experiencing only moderate growth.[11] The congregations should make every effort to complete the unfinished task of making disciples of the whole Grebo tribe— not only the children who go to church schools, but their parents and cousins who live in the villages as well.

Cape Mount and the Port Town Bassa. The Episcopal mission at Cape Mount in the westernmost corner of Liberia demonstrates that the growth of the Church is not necessarily connected with the number and size of institutions operated. As early as 1878 the mission obtained land at Cape Mount for a school. Over the years, American and British missionaries established a boys' school and a girls' school. In 1921 they provided agricultural and industrial training courses, and in 1931 a high school.[12] The schools trained some of the sons of the Vai and Gola tribesmen as well as children of the civilized element in Robertsport. The Vai were largely Muslim, however, among whom there was little church growth. But the importance of this school approach can be illustrated by the fact that one of these Vai boys, T. Momolu Gardner, became a Christian and entered the priesthood. In 1921 he was consecrated Suffragan Bishop— the first tribal man to become Bishop of Liberia.[13] An important individual had become Christian through the school—yet the Church was not growing.

In 1926 a young priest, the late J. D. K. Baker, assigned to St. John's in Cape Mount, realized that his Church and other denominations were ministering to the civilized element, the Vai, and the Gola, but had overlooked the Bassa tribe in that

[9] *Ibid.*, p. 363.
[10] *Ibid.*
[11] Protestant Episcopal Church, *Journal, Thirty-seventh General Convocation,* Robertsport, Liberia, April 27 to May 1, 1960, p. 776; *Journal, Thirty-ninth General Convocation,* Kakata, Liberia, May 2-6, 1962, p. 47.
[12] Cassat, *op. cit.*, p. 56.
[13] *Ibid.*, p. 34.

area. These few hundred Bassa tribesmen were nearly a hundred miles from their tribal homeland near Monrovia, living in the town of Robertsport and laboring as stevedores. Father Baker began working with them and was amazed by their response. The common impression among traders at the time was that the Bassa made good enough stevedores aboard ship but that in port cities they were notorious thieves. Within two years after the first conversion, several traders remarked that the Bassa were more trustworthy. The mission schools, at the time staffed by American missionaries, went right on serving the Vai and the Gola, and the Rev. Mr. Baker went right on evangelizing responsive Bassa.[14] Here was a case, so common in missions around the world, where one element in the society received the services of the mission while a completely different element responded to the Gospel. In this case the Vai and the Gola and the civilized group had their children educated by the mission, but the working-class Bassa, who did not have money enough to pay the fees and whose children did not go to school, were those who responded to the Gospel.

It is interesting to note that about this time Baptist minister Daniel R. Horton was discovering the same kind of eager response among the displaced Bassa laborers in Monrovia. In the tribal homeland of the Bassa, Methodists and Pentecostals as well as the Baptists and Episcopalians at Cape Palmas have been able to establish churches.

We must consider whether a true history of church growth in Liberia outside the Americo-Liberian community is not the ripening and subsequent harvest of one tribe after another—first the Grebo harvested by the Episcopalians at Cape Palmas, then the Kru coming into the Methodist and later the Episcopal Church, then the Bassa (when they were ready to be converted) moving into whatever Church was at hand—Baptist in Monrovia, Methodist and Pentecostal in their homeland, and Episcopal at Cape Mount. Unfortunately, each of these small beginnings of people movements in Liberia barely got under way when it was sealed off. The Church stopped growing before

[14] From an interview with Father J. D. K. Baker, June 1964.

all the tribesmen even heard the Gospel. The evangelization of the whole tribe *as a tribe* was probably never seriously considered.

More recently in Cape Mount the Rev. C. E. Kandakai has had notable response in Vai villages back away from the coast, in what might develop into a movement of that tribe into the Church.[15] The Episcopal Church has shepherded some classic people movements around the world, e.g., in India, Kenya, Uganda. By studying such movements and making a conscious effort to stimulate them, or at least not stand in their way, it is possible that the Episcopalians might expand this growth into a full-fledged movement and sustain it until sizable segments and possibly the whole tribe are affected. In Churches which have highly trained ministers, such as the Episcopalian, rapid growth often stops when the work expands beyond what the one trained priest in the area is capable of supervising. If investigation reveals that conditions for such a movement do exist in the Vai near Cape Mount, then every effort should be made to provide the priest with help. Otherwise the expansion will stop after small churches have been planted in three or four towns. To take advantage of the ripe situation priests, both Liberian and foreign, should be brought in—men who understand people movements and are prepared to work along those lines. Moreover, a second level of village catechist from among the Vai tribesmen should be consecrated—a method used with great success in Anglican dioceses in India[16] and Uganda.

Bolahun in the Northwest Tribes. In 1922 Father Hawkins of the Order of the Holy Cross made a survey of Liberia. He decided to locate a mission of this monastic community at Bolahun, a small village near the Sierra Leone border in the northernmost corner of the country. The government had established full authority in the area just two years earlier by station-

---

[15] *Ibid.*

[16] Harlan P. Beach, ed., *World Missionary Atlas* (New York: Institute of Social and Religious Research, 1925). The Church Missionary Society in Madras, India, one of the great people-movement Churches, had 2,013 such men in 1925 for 58,000 communicant members.

ing a provincial commissioner at Voinjama. The Episcopal monks reached Bolahun by traveling through Sierra Leone and walking from the railhead at Pendembu across the border into Liberia. Because of this, they were not as greatly influenced by the Church in the Americo-Liberian community as other missions in Liberia. The Bolahun mission, moreover, received its support directly from the Order of the Holy Cross in America and was not an integral part of the Episcopal Church and mission in Liberia. Recently the organized congregations of this mission in the towns of Voinjama, Shelloe, and Kolahun have become organized missions of the missionary district of Liberia. The present bishop, the Rt. Rev. Dillard Brown, now travels up country "to confirm members of these congregations at Bolahun."[17]

The English sisters of the community of the Holy Name arrived at Bolahun in 1931 to work with the women and girls. Medical work has also been an integral part of the mission, though a doctor has been in residence only off and on. The circumstances surrounding the mission at Bolahun are so different from those of any other missionary work in Liberia that it is impossible to make valid comparisons. One thing is obvious, however, which is that forty years of work have produced little church growth among the tribal people. There are about 150 adult Kissi villagers who are Episcopal Christians, and there have been only six Loma adults baptized in the past twenty years.[18] Among baptized school children over the same period of time 150 have been confirmed.

The monks have baptized 1,500 persons in the forty years since mission work was begun at Bolahun, 143 of these in the two years from 1960 to 1962. Nearly all were school children who, when they graduated from the school, left the area to go to population centers at nearby Kolahun, Voinjama, or even as far as Monrovia, where job opportunities are available. Some few transfer their membership to congregations in their new home, but many are lost to the Church. In nearby Kolahun, for

[17] From an interview with Father Allen E. Smith, O.H.C., June 1964.
[18] *Ibid.*

example, there are probably twenty-five persons trained at Bolahun (presumably Episcopalians), only five of whom are active in
the congregation there.

Reasons for Slow Growth. So many factors which have been
shown to inhibit the growth of the Church in missions around
the world were also present in the Bolahun mission that it is
difficult to credit lack of growth to any single one.[19] The
monastery is on a high hill overlooking the mission village, or
gathered colony, of Bolahun. The village is small and isolated,
about thirty-five miles from the center of government at Voinjama. Since a base station for missionary activity should be
located at a center of government or of population,[20] this may
have adversely affected growth.

Moreover, the village is located in a corner of the Gbande
tribe, not far from villages of two other tribes: the Loma and
Kissi. Villages of the Mende tribe are also nearby. The fathers
exploring for a site thought that Bolahun would be a "hub from
which Christianity would radiate to the most distant tribesmen."[21] The gathered colony which has grown up at the foot of
the hill where the monastery is located is made up of people from
all three tribes. This has militated against the missionaries' learning any one of the tribal languages. The late Father Bessom
spoke Loma only because he had spent many years in the Loma
village of Vezala, at some distance from the monastery.

The gathered colony of Bolahun became a kind of theocracy.
Until 1964, only Christians or hearers (i.e., those in class) were
allowed to live there. So if a man was willing to leave his own
people and live according to the rules, he could live at Bolahun.
Life there was not without its compensations: it was close to the
hospital, children of the villagers could count on going to
school, jobs were available for most of the able-bodied men, and

[19] See Roland Allen, *The Spontaneous Expansion of the Church*
(London: World Dominion Press, 1956), p. 208, and Donald A.
McGavran, *How Churches Grow* (London: World Dominion
Press, 1959; New York: Friendship Press, 1960), p. 185.

[20] Donald A. McGavran, "Principles and Procedures of Church
Growth," class lecture, Institute of Church Growth, Eugene, Ore.,
1964.

[21] Cassat, *op. cit.*, p. 40.

over the years benevolences worth thousands of dollars were showered down from the monastery on the town below. Until recently, even the thatched roofs of the houses of persons living in the town were repaired by a work crew paid by the mission.

Roland Allen says that this kind of paternalism effectively stops church growth. The gathered colony approach isolates Christians from the pagans in surrounding villages. It is designed to keep their Christianity pure from the world, but by isolating them from the pagans, all natural contacts which could serve as bridges by which the Gospel could pass are lost.[22]

In the existing circumstances, the pagans in surrounding villages are unimpressed by the changed lives of those who live at the colony. The changes in the lives of Christians may be explained away either as the natural result of exotic life in a specially sheltered community or as artificial behavior, a necessary payment for benefits received. Nor are those who receive the benefits anxious to have hundreds of new Christians share them; just as the members of a labor union are not eager to see hundreds of scab laborers compete on an equal basis for their jobs. Thus the gathered colony stands in the way of church growth.

The members of a congregation which pays its own way know that the church belongs to them, and they witness to the faith and encourage others to join with zeal because it is their own.* There is no case of a church supporting its own pastor in the Holy Cross Mission. Even part-time untrained evangelists who get only $3.50 a month are paid out of the treasury of the Order of the Holy Cross.

Many hear the Gospel but stay out of the Church because of the large number of obstacles a new convert must hurdle before being admitted to baptism in this mission. The Holy Cross

[22] Donald A. McGavran, *The Bridges of God* (London: World Dominion Press, 1955; New York: Friendship Press, 1956), p. 158.

* The relation of self-support to the pastoral concern of the ministry is discussed in Chapter VIII, p. 185.

fathers require the longest catechumenate (four years' preparation before baptism) of any Church or mission in Liberia. A person who wishes to become a Christian first becomes a hearer, who must attend services once a week and classes regularly. The first two years are spent in a study of monotheism as a preparation for the coming to Christ. At the end of this period the hearer receives a wooden cross and becomes a catechumen at a service in which he promises:

1. I will not go to the diviner.
2. I will not use country medicine.
3. I will not offer sacrifices, except God's own.
4. I will not eat foods that have been given in sacrifices, except God's own.
5. I will keep God's law for marriage.

Then follow two years during which the catechumen must live an exemplary life and study the life of our Lord, before he is baptized. In effect, the believer is expected to live an exemplary life without the help and assurance of grace which baptism provides. And he must make his way as an individual seeker. He is not approached as a man-in-society, a member of family and clan, but strictly as an individual. The first wife of a polygamous household can be baptized. Until 1964, other wives could become catechumens only. Husbands of polygamous households are denied baptism. This is not something the Holy Cross fathers can do much about, since it is a general rule of discipline of the Episcopal Church.

There is some evidence that after many years of hearing the Gospel proclaimed, the population is willing to respond. The barrier of the catechumenate has discouraged all but a few spiritual athletes, and students who went through the preparation as a matter of course in their school, from joining the Church. Fortunately, the northernmost tribes share in a general ripening, brought about in large measure no doubt by the faithful labors of the fathers. The Roman Catholics and Swedish Pentecostals have recognized this responsive population and have built churches in Kolahun and Voinjama and elsewhere in the territory. Churches and missions are channels of

God's grace to lost man. If one channel is blocked for some reason or other, God will find a way to save His children, even if He has to go around that channel or use some other Church to reach them.

I have spoken frankly of the problems of church growth at Bolahun because members of the staff—monks, nuns, and laymen—have themselves spoken openly and frankly about them to me. The missionary staff at Bolahun is aware of the lack of church growth. What is even more unsettling to them is the fact that after forty years there has not been a single Liberian vocation—no tribesman has become a monk, nun, or priest (though two are now studying for the priesthood). Father Allen Smith told me, "In other parts of Africa hundreds have become nuns and monks, and priests."[23] The staff is earnestly and sincerely examining the policies and practices of their mission, daring to question even the basic techniques of their work in prayer.

Since 1964 the fathers have taken some steps to correct the paternalism of the past. The town has been turned over to the townspeople. They now govern their own affairs. In the past they had no voice in the governing of the mission. Now evangelism, medical, and school committees have been formed and participate in planning the activities of the mission. This willingness to face painful questions and experiment with new methods is a harbinger of new possibilities for growth. The problems faced by a gathered colony mission like Bolahun in striving to initiate rapid church growth of the people movement type is well described by Dr. McGavran in *Bridges of God:*

1. The gathered church must accept group ingathering as a desirable form of church growth and learn its pattern.

2. They should concentrate their attention on some one people which they deem most winnable.

3. They must accept clan and tribe as instruments of evangelism and stop trying to desocialize their converts.

4. They must convert enough individuals and groups of the winnable people quickly enough so that each convert comes into

[23] Smith interview.

the church with some of his kindred. When this takes place, a people movement is under way.[24]

The "hard core" Christians prepared at Bolahun over the years can be the yeast for evangelizing a single sector of the total population in the Bolahun area if they can get out into the whole society.

Americo-Liberians in Monrovia. The Episcopal Church entered Monrovia in 1851. Today there are three Episcopalian churches in the city. The largest, Trinity Cathedral, has a baptized membership of more than 1,200 persons. It is completely self-supporting and by itself is larger than several whole denominations at work in the republic. Its members are involved in many activities. One group calls on the sick and shut-ins while another visits hospitals and prisons. They have a day school with 700 students and a Sunday school of over 400; also several youth groups, a girls' friendly society, and Boy Scouts. The congregation supports the leper colony at Cape Mount and has sent gifts for work at Bassa, Kakata, and Nimba. Of special interest to us is the pattern of church growth that has emerged—a technique for multiplying churches in the city of Monrovia itself.

In this plan, members of the congregation go out to the crowded slum areas of the city to start Sunday schools and churches for people who live too far from the cathedral to attend, or who might feel out of place among the well-dressed, highly educated congregation there. At present two Sunday schools meet in public school buildings at Bushrod and West Point. The deacon at Trinity Cathedral, the Rev. Burgess Carr, is training lay leaders who will be able to lead matins and vesper services in these small congregations that have no priest.[25]

The other large congregation in Monrovia, St. Thomas, is itself the result of such an effort. The late Dr. J. D. K. Baker, when rector of that congregation, told me, "The congregation I now serve was started in old Kru town. The people of Kru town were pagans and lived in debauchery. A group of faithful

[24] McGavran, *Bridges of God,* p. 129.
[25] Carr interview.

church women directed by the Rev. N. H. B. Cassell and an outstanding layman, Mr. Ogee, started Sunday school for Kru children in the area. St. Thomas emerged from that work. St. Thomas is no longer a Kru church but its members come from all parts of town and from all walks of life."[26]

Interestingly enough, St. Thomas is reaching out in several mission projects of its own, including support of a mission in the Bong mine area. Only rarely do Trinity Cathedral and St. Thomas receive members by adult baptism. These congregations are growing slowly but steadily among the second generation by infant baptism and confirmation. However, they have demonstrated that rapid growth of the Church can take place in the city through a plan for multiplying new congregations.

These two congregations are planting churches across cultural barriers in Monrovia. Other denominations should see that such growth is possible and do their share in shepherding the thousands of unchurched in Monrovia.

Polity. Like most of the major denominations in Liberia, the Episcopal Church is working out new organizational relationships which may affect stability and growth in the future. The first step is to become a diocese in itself instead of a missionary district of a North American diocese. According to Protestant Episcopal practice, this requires six self-supporting parishes. In 1964 there were only four. After six have achieved self-support, the Episcopal Church in Liberia will move in one of three directions: it may become (a) an independent diocese of the Protestant Episcopal Church in the United States, or (b) the Episcopal Church in Liberia, or (c) a diocese of the Anglican Province of West Africa, i.e., Sierra Leone through Nigeria.

This last is the most likely course, but one about which Liberian churchmen have the deepest reservations. The Liberian Church is like an island with American connections, surrounded by the Province of the Anglican Church with British connections in the rest of West Africa. While Liberians have no serious objections to becoming part of the Province, a hundred years of Protestant Episcopal—i.e., American—traditions cannot easily be overturned. The fear that those traditions will be lost in

---

[26] Baker interview.

joining the Province of West Africa is understandable, since the Liberian diocese with only nine thousand members would be joining a province of nearly eighty thousand members.[27]

Statistics. Perhaps a word is in order here about the statistics presented in these descriptions of the Churches. For example, the 10 per cent increase per year of the Episcopalian Church, sustained over a decade, largely among the Americo-Liberians, is healthy growth. But since this percentage is based on field totals, it may conceal as much of the real situation as it reveals.

The individual congregations in the Monrovia subdistrict represent a variety of situations—different levels of pastoral care, different economic status of the people, different tribes, and different social and cultural patterns. In the two-year period from 1960 to 1962, one of these congregations grew more than 100 per cent, increasing its membership from 80 to 177. The congregation at Bomi Hills, on the other hand, in the same two-year period reported a loss of 17—decreasing from 40 to 23 communicant members. Church administrators and those who are interested in the growth of the Church should not be content with field total comparisons, but rather examine carefully the growth in each individual congregation. Only by observing both the circumstances and the statistics can we come to valid conclusions concerning the effectiveness of a given program of evangelism or a method that has been used in a congregation. The Episcopalians are perhaps more careful about reporting statistics than any other Church in the country, yet even with such care situations sometimes come to light which cast doubt on the reliability of figures.

For instance, in 1962 it was reported: "After a careful check on the list of members in some of the stations and in the parish it was revealed that there are members who have registered in two or three places, and the same name of one man is carried in all three places. There is a man who was confirmed in Rocktown, moved to Pleebo and registered his membership without transfer, then went on to Webbo and registered his membership

[27] Carr interview.

there."[28] The fact that such situations come to light and are faithfully corrected commends the statistics of the Episcopal Church. Some denominations are unable to give figures at all. This handicaps missionaries and workers who seek to make an objective evaluation of a given situation. Poor, and even harmful, evangelistic methods which produce no fruits are continued year after year because no objective reference can be made to the results in church expansion which did or did not take place. Vice President William R. Tolbert recently urged leaders of the Liberian Baptist Convention to make a concerted effort to record and report accurate statistics.[29] This is one thing that will surely contribute to intelligent planning for the growth of the Church.

THE LUTHERAN CHURCH

Beginnings at Muhlenberg. The Lutheran Church in Liberia is unique among the older missions in that from the beginning it chose to work exclusively among the tribal people.[30] In 1860 Morris Officer, a Lutheran pastor, was sent out from the United States as a missionary by the General Synod. He chose a site on the St. Paul River just a few miles farther inland than the most interior settlement of the time, and called the mission Muhlenberg after Henry Melchior Muhlenberg, the first German missionary to the United States. The primary criterion he used in choosing the site was that it should be a place where no other Church or mission was working. Carrying out this original purpose has made planting the Church a slow and expensive process for the Lutherans. The Lutheran Church today has more missionaries than any other Church or mission in Liberia, where its total enterprise receives more foreign subsidy ($450,000 in 1964, not counting the $2,500,000 capital invest-

[28] Protestant Episcopal Church, *Journal, Thirty-ninth General Convocation*, p. 38.
[29] Letter to the author from Augustus B. Marwieh, May 16, 1965.
[30] Whetstone, *Lutheran Mission in Liberia*, p. 217.

ment in the Phoebe Hospital) than any other two Churches in the republic.[31]

Morris Officer began by building a school, but the tribal people in the area refused to send their children. Another possibility presented itself when an American man-of-war cruising near the mouth of the Congo River captured a slave ship and brought its cargo to Liberia to be released. Officer asked for and obtained twenty boys and twenty girls released into the custody of the Lutheran mission. Thus the pitiful immediate victims of the slave trade were the first beneficiaries of Lutheran mission work in Liberia. They were brought into a Christian colony where they could be taught "the virtues of religion and civilization."[32] The life of the mission revolved around this orphanage. Later it became the central boarding school for children of the indigenous tribes. Some children were secured by the then common system of indenturing. The missionaries argued that since the indigenous tribesmen would not send their children to school without payment, it was obviously better to get them for a small price than not to get them at all.

By 1874 there was a small Christian community with forty families and fifty-five baptized members around the Muhlenberg station. With a school at its center and education as its purpose, this community was supplemented by branch schools in other villages. Through the years, education remained the main effort of the Lutheran mission. Schools had first claim on staff and money. Schools were started in villages where no congregation existed—in fact, even before a single person was baptized. It was the plan to work through the young people in the schools and thus Christianize the tribes. But the plan did not succeed. Yet it continued to determine policy, since it was based on theory arising from the conviction that Christian life required such a profound change from "the savage animism of the natives" that only long years of education in a controlled

[31] Lutheran Church in Liberia, Treasurer's Report, January 1965. Mimeographed.
[32] Whetstone, op. cit., p. 19.

Christian environment could enable tribesmen to live as real Christians.[33]

The Lutheran mission was on the edge of the confrontation between Western civilization in the America-Liberian communities and the tribal culture, a kind of buffer between the two. The encounter was defined and took place in the school. The missionaries made some trips to the villages preaching through an interpreter, and later sent older schoolboys out to the villages to preach, but most missionary time and effort was spent in the school. The task of making disciples was identified with "educating and civilizing the natives." This concept was easier to hold because of the proximity of the America-Liberian community.

None of the early colonists were Lutherans. The General Synod had no work in the southern states in America, and indeed there were scarcely any Negro Lutherans in the United States. The Lutherans, therefore, had no civilized leadership to take over and operate a Liberian Church. The orphan slaves and village children, after spending six or eight years in the mission schools, gravitated toward the America-Liberian settlements, where they joined Methodist, Baptist, and Presbyterian* community churches. So the leadership of the Lutheran Church fell to the foreign missionaries, and one of the reasons it grew so slowly was that it was wholly dominated by and dependent upon them. Even today, in 1966, there are more ordained missionaries than Liberian pastors in the Lutheran Church in Liberia.

The colonists in the other denominations were unalterably committed to staying in Liberia and provided leadership and continuity for the life of the congregations. There were very few Lutheran missionaries in the early years; indeed, for five of those years there were none at all. Those who did come seldom remained more than a year or two. Nine of the first twenty-two

---

[33] *Ibid.*, p. 29.

* Presbyterians as a mission force ceased to exist sometime later, though today there is a Presbyterian Church in Monrovia with a membership of some hundreds. Hence Presbyterian mission labors are not treated.

men sent to Liberia by the Lutheran Church died on the field.
One, however, missionary Rev. David A. Day, and his wife did
provide the continuity so necessary for church growth in those
early years. They served for twenty-three years. During much
of that time they were the only Lutheran missionaries in Liberia. With such a small staff and the school-centered approach,
it is not surprising that in 1922, after sixty years of Lutheran
work, the Church had a baptized membership of only 192, less
than a tenth of the total number of students who had gone
through the Lutheran schools in the meantime. The Lutherans
sustained these great losses because they did not organize their
converts into congregations of an indigenous Church. Except
for the congregation at Muhlenberg, no churches were established in the settlements, and only small churches in the tribal
villages. David Day did have a plan for establishing an indigenous, self-supporting Church. He developed a coffee plantation that netted $4,984.57 for the mission in the two years
between 1893 and 1895. He ordained the first two Lutheran
pastors—David Davidson, a Congolese, in 1885 and Joseph
Stewart, a Gola tribesman, in 1892. Stewart was a zealous
church planter.[34] But both these pastors died a few years after
their ordination, and church growth ceased.

In 1887 a native chief, Ben Moore, burned his fetishes and
the village "devil bush" and became a licensed evangelist. A
movement developed, and several congregations were organized
within a ten-mile radius of the Muhlenberg station. In one town
the local Christians contributed $86.10 to build a church. Day
said, "I would rather have this one little church built and
supported by themselves than a dozen built and supported with
money from home. Our whole aim has been to help them help
themselves."[35]

Undoubtedly his feelings about the importance of self-
support were shared by other missionaries, but the policy was
not firmly stated, and there was such a rapid turnover of
personnel that the Lutheran mission seems to have lost sight of
this guiding principle. A congregation might struggle for a few

[34] *Ibid.*, p. 33.
[35] Cason, *op. cit.*, p. 283.

years on its own, but then a new missionary (intending to help) would arrange for money from abroad and would build them a nice big church. Thus the initiative would revert to the missionaries. The development of an indigenous church was almost impossible in the face of such insistent help and support. Many evangelists over the years, both ex-schoolboys and tribal men, have started preaching and holding services in one town or another on their own—without pay. But as soon as a missionary discovered a "free-time" worker, he would put the fellow on the payroll with the rest of the evangelists. Unity and lines of authority were well preserved, but one can hardly imagine a more effective way of smothering the spontaneous expansion of the Church.[36]

Expansion to the Tribes. As soon as the government established effective control over the interior and it was safe for missionaries to travel, the Lutherans expanded away from the coast. The Muhlenberg pattern was repeated in a chain of five Lutheran stations across the middle of Liberia in the St. Paul River valley. At each new location a mission compound developed, centered around a school apart from the village. The first missionary was stationed at Kpolopele in 1908. This is sixty-five miles up the St. Paul River from Muhlenberg. The Muhlenberg station was located in territory occupied by the Gola and Bassa tribes, but this new move brought the Lutherans into contact with a new tribe, the Kpelle. After 1925 the last outstation in the Gola tribe was closed, and the Lutherans determined to serve the Kpelle and Loma tribes exclusively. In 1917 a missionary took up residence in another Kpelle town, Sanoyea, about 110 miles from Muhlenberg by jungle path. An orphanage was operated at this station from 1939 to 1961, and a large dispensary and midwifery clinic is there today. In 1923 a station was opened at Zorzor, just three miles from the Guinea border. This chain of stations was strengthened by the addition of Bellefanai, between Zorzor and Sanoyea, in 1932. The pattern of church growth at all the stations was based almost exclusively on individual accessions among the school pupils and

[36] From an interview with the Rev. Louis T. Bowers, June 1965.

English-speaking mission employees. Thus, although the Lutherans made a conscious decision to carry the Gospel to the "tribes only," in actual practice their converts became just as much separated from the tribal villagers by education and culture as were the settlers. The villagers who had never been to school nor worked for the mission did not even consider Christianity as a real option for themselves.

Today the Lutheran Church operates nine grade schools with nearly 1,000 pupils and 50 teachers.[37] In 1953 the high school was moved to the interior, Salayea, eighteen miles from Zorzor, near the border between the Loma and Kpelle tribes. The buildings at the old Muhlenberg station have been turned over to the government. A church of 119 baptized members is all that remains of the Lutheran work there.

It must not be imagined that Lutheran activity at these stations was exclusively educational. Evangelistic and medical work were also carried on. Education was never considered more important than evangelism, but it was accepted as the best means by which "making disciples" could be accomplished. Sometimes, too, education became an end in itself.

Medical work was an important part of the Lutheran effort in Liberia. In 1896 the first doctor came to Muhlenberg. In 1921 a hospital was built there; and a nurses' training school, the first in the republic, was opened that same year. Dispensaries were operated at all the stations as soon as trained personnel were available. A hospital was opened at Zorzor station in 1924, and in 1944 the Curran Memorial Hospital was built and the nurses' training school moved there. In 1965 the Lutherans completed a $2,500,000 hospital at Suokoko, across the road from Cuttington College. This new location is nearer the center of the area where rapid growth of the Lutheran Church has taken place.

Nor was medical work ever intended to be an alternative to evangelism, either. Originally all three phases of mission work—education, medicine, and evangelism, and indeed the literacy program also—were meant to be part of an integrated witness

[37] Evangelical Lutheran Church in Liberia, "Pre-Convention Bulletin of Reports, E.L.C.L.," 1963. Mimeographed.

to the Lord of the Church. In actual practice the work often becomes departmentalized. Missionaries are specialists, each responsible for his particular realm and concerned with departmental problems. The necessarily limited funds are coveted for departmental projects. Where personnel are interchangeable (for example, a pastor may be the principal of the school or supervisor of evangelistic work in surrounding villages), the institution invariably takes precedence. Training Liberians to take over jobs at the administrative level, especially in education, has relieved this situation but not completely solved it.

A New Pattern of Growth. In the village of Sanoyea in 1927, missionary David A. Dagel baptized the first tribal convert in the Lutheran area who was neither a schoolboy nor a mission employee. The man's name was Somo Yakbors, and he became an evangelist. He was later dismissed because he could not read English. But he was the first. Pastor Dagel continued to baptize small groups of tribal people in several towns and villages around Sanoyea, though in fact few were baptized in Sanoyea itself.[38]

It is important to recognize that these baptisms constituted a new pattern of church growth—a real innovation. For years only the schoolboys and a few mission workers had been baptized. With this innovation the missionaries, the Christian community, and the tribal people began learning a new way of becoming a Christian. The individual still had to leave his society and come by himself. An evangelist could be released for not knowing how to read English. But becoming a Christian was no longer limited to those who had spent long years in school, learning to speak English and read books. A new plan was developing. Missionaries were realizing that God's grace and mercy are available even for those who are too old to go to school. By 1939 this new pattern had evidently been generally accepted, for missionary Louis Bowers reports that in that year he baptized thirty in the village of Kpolopele and fourteen in Parakwele on a single trip.[39]

[38] Bowers interview.
[39] *Ibid.*

The baptism of unschooled villagers must not be interpreted as a lowering of Christian standards, but rather as a disentangling of Christianity from Western culture. In fact, the social pressures and threats which the villager endures in becoming a Christian constitute a greater sacrifice for his faith than those the schoolboy makes, who becomes a Christian in the relatively sheltered surroundings of the mission compound. When Bowers, for example, went across the St. Paul River to Parakwele in answer to the call of the evangelist there, he found fourteen men ready for baptism. The whole town turned out to see the service. When the time came for the baptisms, the *zo* or fetish priest stood up and declared, "I forbid these men to be baptized." Then, turning to the men, he announced, "If you let this man baptize you, you will be dead by this time tomorrow." The men were surprised, and Bowers told them it was up to them. "You know Christ," he said. They went outside and had a meeting to decide. After five minutes they came back and said, "Baptize us. If we die, we will be with Jesus." When the service was over, the *zo* came to Bowers secretly and said, "Tell me about this Jesus. His power is greater than mine."[40]

Ten years later this pattern of growth hit a new stride around the town of Totota, in the Sanoyea parish, one of those on the road. Near Sanoyea the growth had been scattered, Christian groups were baptized in certain towns, with two or three towns intervening where no converts were made. In the Totota area, however, the Church grew in one town after the other—from nothing in 1947 to 850 in 1955. All the rest of the Lutheran Church added only 410 baptisms in that eight-year period.[41] The Totota region was obviously a responsive section of the population. Fortunately, the Lutherans recognized the potential and concentrated their efforts there. As membership increased, the parishes were divided and redivided. Missionaries and later Liberian pastors were stationed in this area to disciple the responsive groups.

Stationing enough ordained pastors in this region to shepherd new converts and speed the expansion has been an important

---

[40] *Ibid.*
[41] *Ibid.*

factor in the rapid growth of the Church there. But it has grown also in the more isolated sections of Parakwele, where until 1965 no pastor had been stationed. This shows that an even more important factor in church growth than a resident pastor is that the pattern of church planting be understood and carried out by village evangelists. The Lutheran Church has more than 200 such workers.

Pastor Bowers tells of one evangelist named Taipon who had a zeal to plant churches. He would pick out a town where there was no church and start preaching there. In a few months he would come and report the number of people ready for baptism. As soon as Pastor Bowers was able to take over the supervision of the work, Taipon would move on to another village. Interestingly enough, the town of Totota itself was the last to have a church, though the school and missionary residences were located there. If rigorous church planting had not been done in the surrounding towns and villages, the excellent mission work in Totota would have continued sterile in the midst of an area of high potential. This has happened frequently in other places in Liberia.

Reasons for Growth. Several factors made the time auspicious for rapid church growth.

1. In 1947 the Evangelical Lutheran Church in Liberia was organized, and some leaders began thinking of the Church as their own.

2. In 1948 Frank Laubach came to Liberia, and the literacy program really caught on. Suddenly there were hundreds of literates able to read materials in their own language, including parts of the Bible.

3. That same year Dr. Welmers completed his Kpelle grammar and D. Wesley Saddler wrote his teaching grammar for the Loma language. Scientific and systematic language study by all missionary pastors dates from that period. Today the Lutheran literacy program in the Kpelle and Loma languages is one of the best in all Africa.[42] Missionary Otto Spehr and John

[42] From an interview with Dr. Wesley Saddler, then director of the Literacy and Literature Center at Kitwe, Northern Rhodesia, January 1961.

McKay have completed the translation of the Kpelle New Testament. The Rev. Gerald E. Currens and Mr. Yella Quaqua are completing an excellent translation of the New Testament into Loma. Regular periodicals and literacy materials are mimeographed in both languages.

4. In 1949 the missionary at Totota "started permitting the people to sing hymns to native tunes in the worship services."[43]

To what extent each of these factors contributed to the growth of the Church it is impossible to say. Perhaps more important than their individual effect, they reflect an identification of the Church with the people—an identification so strong that even the missionaries recognized it and began to change their own attitudes and activities to fit the new pattern. There are some villages where growth never did start, and others where it got started and stopped. In a few villages the growth has continued until Christians are now in the majority. Villagers have hacked twenty-two air strips out of the forest, so that pastors can visit congregations by plane. In 1962 four Liberian pastors finished their training at Lutheran Training Institute in Salayea and were ordained as ministers. These men, too, understood the new pattern by which the Church could grow. Only Rev. B. L. Byepu was stationed in the center of the area of rapid expansion, at Sanoyea. The others were located on the periphery where rapid growth had not yet taken place—but it soon did. In Salayea, for example, where services had been held for many years, supervised by a missionary as a secondary assignment, there was a congregation of 35. Before the year was out, Pastor Mulbah Jackson had gathered a congregation of 250.[44]

The pattern of church growth did not immediately cross tribal lines. Work in the Loma tribe in these years did not produce the same kind of growth that was taking place near Totota. The Loma people still thought of becoming a Christian as a process of alienation from their tribe. Whether lack of growth was due to mission policies or to a natural time lag is

[43] Bowers interview.
[44] From an interview with the Rev. Mulbah Jackson, April 1964.

uncertain. This station was opened later, and the Loma tribe was farther away from the coast and had had less contact with the Americo-Liberians. At any rate, growth did not take place. There were 460 baptized members in the Loma district in 1948. In 1950 they reported 768. But two years later, after a culling of the rolls, only 268 Christians could be found in the district.[45]

These losses do not necessarily reflect backsliders, but rather the mobility of the population. Large numbers of young men were leaving the area and "going down" to Monrovia and Firestone to find work. These were the very ones who had been willing to be baptized while they remained in the village. They were a leaven in the whole lump of society, but since they were almost entirely young men without other members of their families, when they went away they took the church with them, leaving the villages solidly pagan. In recent years, however, the Loma people too have begun to respond favorably to the Gospel. The Totota pattern of baptisms for a cross section of the population has been established. The Church in this district has grown from 283 in 1956 to 1,192 in 1964, or an average of 50 per cent increase per year.[46] The evidence indicates that these southern "clans" of the Loma tribe are ready for harvest.

There are other instances where a rapid growth potential is being realized. But the people movement type of growth that has marked Lutheran work in New Guinea, parts of India, and Tanzania, when it comes in Liberia, will make these little spurts seem fitful and hesitant indeed.

The excellent literacy program and New Testament translations in Kpelle and Loma have set the stage for a sound training and solid shepherding of the masses of unschooled villagers. But until the Lutherans make hard, bold plans for church planting and implement them along sound anthropological

[45] Lutheran Mission in Liberia, "Minutes of the Twenty-second Annual Conference," 1948; "Minutes of the Twenty-fourth Annual Conference," 1950; and "Minutes of the Twenty-sixth Annual Conference," 1952. Mimeographed.

[46] Evangelical Lutheran Church in Liberia, "Minutes of the Tenth Biennial Convention of the E.L.C.L., Statistical Report." Mimeographed.

lines, the literacy program is like a stage set without actors. The translations are unread—scripts gathering dust on a shelf.

I am here warning against complacency. At a time when rapid expansion of the Church is a real possibility, we cannot be content with a mission program based on fixed institutions which do not meet the needs of the people. Institutions, for all their cost and fine administration, are not the Church, and do not even serve the Church if they are out of touch with it.

Urban-Industrial Opportunities. The Lutheran Church is a rural Church. It has grown almost exclusively in the villages and towns of the Kpelle and Loma tribes. Only five per cent of its members reside in what can be called urban areas. But large numbers of the tribal people have "gone down" to the urban industrial centers to seek employment. A new phase of Lutheran expansion has begun in efforts to minister to Lutheran members in the urban situation. In 1954 St. Peter's congregation was organized in Monrovia to minister to Lutheran workers and students in that area. In 1963 and 1964 steps were taken to establish churches for the Lutherans working at the mining centers of Bomi, Bong and Nimba. Beginning in 1958 pastors from the Loma district made monthly visits to Bomi to hold services for local Christians. A Kpelle evangelist, Peter Giddings, carried on the work, and in 1964 a missionary pastor, Ronald Kragthorpe, took up residence there. Two missionaries who have recently finished language study will also be stationed in urban industrial centers. One speaks German and will organize a congregation with the German-speaking Lutherans at the Bong mine, as well as Kpelle and Loma tribal workers, while the other will serve the Swedish Lutheran community and tribal workers at Mt. Nimba. The Church is exploring an interdenominational arrangement that will make it possible to form congregations among the Loma and Kpelle communities on the Firestone plantation, where hundreds of baptized Lutherans now reside.

Firestone company policy forbids denominations from organizing congregations or building church buildings on the plantation. But community church buildings are too far and too few to serve the tribal workers and their families.[47] The policy was

[47] From an interview with Firestone management, March 1964.

understandable at a time when almost none of the workers in the labor camps were Christians. But now, when even their families in the villages upcountry are moving into the Church, this rule denies the plantation workers the basic right to worship in their own churches, according to their choice.

Self-Government. The Lutheran missionaries, like those in other missions working exclusively among the tribal Liberians, were sometimes tempted to deprecate the culture of the Americo-Liberians, taking the side of the tribal man in the face of social injustices to which he is subjected. Thus the missionaries tended to isolate themselves and their work from the mainstream of Liberian culture. Charges that the Lutheran Church was exclusive and self-contained were not entirely unjustified. This attitude will very likely disappear in the near future, as Liberians emerge to provide leadership. As has already been mentioned, the Evangelical Lutheran Church in Liberia was formed in 1947. This established a national church, but the Lutheran mission continued to exist. In effect, there were two Lutheran bodies functioning in Liberia side by side. The duplication of committees and multiplication of committee meetings convinced everyone involved that this situation should be temporary. In 1965, after years of planning during which constitutions were written and rewritten, the Evangelical Lutheran Church in Liberia became the Lutheran Church in Liberia, and the Lutheran mission passed out of existence.

Roland J. Payne, president of the new Church, is the son of a paramount chief. He put himself through high school and went to Midland Lutheran College in the United States, returning then to Liberia, where for five years he was secretary of the Church while serving on a staff of the Lutheran hospital in Zorzor. Then he went to seminary in Canada, and was elected president of the Evangelical Lutheran Church on his return. Equally at home speaking to a village congregation in either the Kpelle or Loma language, leading a business session of the Church in convention, or representing his Church in an international ecumenical gathering, Pastor Payne is a symbol of the new Lutheran Church in Liberia and an example of the capable young churchmen who are emerging into the leadership of all the denominations. At a time when both Loma and

Kpelle are beginning to turn to Christ in large numbers, the Lutheran Church is fortunate to have a leader who speaks both languages and understands the importance of the growth of the Church. His major task may well be to organize the Church and so spend his own energies that, in this generation, a church is planted in every Loma and Kpelle village in Liberia.

THE ROMAN CATHOLIC CHURCH

Roman Catholic missions had trouble getting started in Liberia. Bishop Barron's mission from America in 1843 ended in failure. In the 1880's two missionaries of the Holy Ghost Fathers began a school and church in Monrovia. But opposition forced them to withdraw, and the mission was closed in 1887. In 1903, three Montfort Fathers attempted a mission, but sickness and death led them to abandon their work in 1904. Finally in 1906 the Society of African Missions was asked to take charge. Their efforts resulted in a permanent planting of the Church. The Roman Catholic Church in Liberia today is an outgrowth of their mission.

Several stations were opened, including those at Monrovia and Kakata, but in 1909 a young Kru tribesman, Tom Nimine, who had worked with Roman Catholics in Lagos, Nigeria, asked the fathers to visit Sasstown. On a second visit in 1911 the priests found the people open and receptive. The Roman Catholics closed their stations at Monrovia and Kakata and concentrated their efforts on the Kru coast. In 1915 they reported 100 students and 500 catechumens, and the beginnings of translation into Kru.[48] The Kru tribe was ripe, and the Roman Catholics were harvesting them. At the same time, Walter Williams in the Methodist mission was also experiencing phenomenal growth among the Kru. Here again a tribe was ready to change its religion and was not particular about the denomination into which it moved. By 1920, as a result of the Roman Catholic mission, there were 2,400 communicants and 5,594

[48] Martin J. Bane, *The Catholic Story of Liberia* (New York: D. X. McMullen Co., 1950), p. 89.

catechumens, 12 European priests and 10 centers of work—10 schools with 15 teachers and 1,200 pupils.[49]

In that year some members of the Liberian Senate debated a resolution to cut short Roman Catholic mission work in the country, but they were dissuaded by the Vice President, the Hon. Wesley Toh. Although Liberia is a predominantly Protestant nation, the Roman Catholic Church has taken advantage of the relation of Church and state there in a way that no other denomination has. In the thirties, when other denominations were withdrawing their support and forcing Liberians to depend upon themselves, the Roman Catholic Church increased both funds and priests from abroad. Stations were opened at Bassa in 1929, Cape Palmas in 1930, Sanokwele near the Guinea border in 1932, and Gbaraga in 1933,[50] with 14 outstations and schools. At this same time a number of governments were withdrawing recognition of Liberia because of the report of the League of Nations concerning slave labor, but the Vatican gave diplomatic support and a vote of confidence to the struggling nation in this difficult period by elevating Liberia (which had been a prefecture) to the status of vicariate apostolic. This did much to change anti-Catholic feeling into favorable reaction in the country.[51] Today Liberia has two bishops and is divided into two vicariates. Further expansion has taken place, with the establishment of a mission at Tchien in 1958 and a station at Voinjama, so that today the Roman Catholic Church has the most thorough geographic coverage of the country of any mission its size.[52]

The most recent papal encyclical on missions states:

> It is not enough to convert people in young Christian congregations to the Catholic faith and to register them after baptism in large numbers in the church files. They must under all circumstances receive a Christian education which is suitable to the local situation at the present time and which will

[49] Cason, *op. cit.*, p. 380.

[50] *Ibid.*, p. 382.

[51] *Ibid.*, p. 140.

[52] From an interview with Father P. Burgess, First Secretary, Internunciature Apostolic, June 1964.

enable them—according to their ability—to take on such
tasks as are of value for the well being and growth of the
church in present and future.[53]

The policy of the Roman Catholic mission in Liberia adheres to
this general policy statement. All stations emphasize schools and
provide a thorough education for the students. When a new
station is opened, the procedure followed is first to build a
school, then a church, and finally a rectory for the priest. At
present each station is manned by at least one priest. Expatriate
missionaries outnumber the native clergy. St. Theresa's school
for girls was started in 1936, St. Patrick's High School in 1941,
both in Monrovia. Our Lady of Fatima College and high school
for teacher training was opened in 1953 in Cape Palmas. The
Roman Catholic Church has a workable plan whereby priests
go to Nigeria for their training. In 1946 the first Liberian priest
was ordained, and in 1959 the first Liberian nun took her vows.
There are eight Liberian priests and seven sisters in training.

Historically the Roman Catholic Church is no stranger to the
people movement pattern of church growth, but in Liberia, with
the exception of the early expansion on the Kru coast, Roman
Catholics have not experienced any rapid ingathering. Most
growth takes place slowly by individual accessions from among
the school students.

THE PENTECOSTAL CHURCHES

Nine Assemblies of God missionaries from both the United
States and Canada arrived in Liberia on Christmas Day in
1908. J. M. Perkins, leader of the group, and one other had
been Methodist missionaries who received the "baptism of the
Holy Spirit" while home on furlough and returned to Liberia
under new auspices. Like the Lutherans, the Assemblies of God
made a conscious decision to go to the tribes of the interior
instead of to the English-speaking communities in the settlements.[54]

[53] Hugo Schnell, "Mission Strategy of the Roman Catholic
Church," *World Encounter*, Vol. 1, No. 2 (December 1963), p.
8.

[54] Cason, *op. cit.*, p. 296.

When they landed at Garoway they met Jasper Toe, a Christian of the Baroba tribe who was prayerfully seeking someone to bring the Gospel to his people. The missionaries walked two days to reach his home town of Newaka in the interior, and there they planted a church. Notable baptisms took place during a revival in 1913, but 1916 "marks the date of the first real pentecostal outpouring of the Holy Spirit in Liberia." Even enemies of the faith were converted. There were some Christians who healed physical ailments as well as spoke in tongues. The Assemblies of God expanded to Putu in 1921 and further into the interior to Tchien in 1929. In 1930 they opened their first mission station on the coast at Cape Palmas, and in 1937 another congregation was established at Greenville in Sinoe County.[55]

Efforts to evangelize Tiehnpo in 1928 resulted in a great persecution of the Christians in which some were martyred by their fellow tribesmen. But in the revivals between 1926 and 1936 over a thousand people confessed Christ.

In order to comply with the requirements of the Liberian Government, the early missionaries established boarding schools, taking from fifty to ninety students into each mission compound situation. In 1931, however, work was begun at Jadapoo on a different basis, its sole aim being to evangelize the people. Government requirements were met, but only by the establishment of day schools. The missionaries did not assume responsibility for supporting any students, and a strong native Church resulted from the work there. Today the area where the Assemblies of God mission has been at work is the only place in Liberia where whole villages of tribal people have burned their fetishes. It is the one place in Liberia where a person can walk from one town or village to another without seeing *juju* in any of them. There are villages where nearly the whole population turns out for Sunday evening services.[56]

In 1964 twenty-six of the thirty-five Assemblies of God missionaries in the country were working in the Cape Palmas di-

[55] *Ibid.*
[56] From an interview with the Rev. H. H. Landrus.

vision. There were also churches in Monrovia and a Bible school at Brewerville. In the Cape Palmas division were 152 ministers and 27 other workers who had been trained at five Bible schools operated by the mission; also 150 organized churches, and three preaching points. Miss Katie Jean Jones, the divisional secretary, writes, "Our active adult membership stands at 3,932. Other believers number 8,890. Of these members 1,353 have been baptized in the Holy Spirit in addition to their water baptism. Sunday school enrollment is 3,825. . . . All our churches are on an indigenous basis, and the pastors are all supported by the people whom they serve. All interior pastors make rice farms to supplement their income." These men receive an average of three to five dollars a month, taken out of the offerings and tithes.[57]

The Bible schools at Pleebo and Owens Grove are located near the Firestone rubber plantations. Students who enter with third-grade training are expected to support themselves as rubber tappers and attend classes from 3:30 to 9 p.m. Three other Bible schools train workers in other areas. Congregations are on their own as soon as they are organized. The church government is entirely in the hands of Liberians. Decisions as to who will be baptized are determined by local church councils in consultations with the missionaries. The Assemblies of God mission was the first to bring airplanes to Liberia (1945) and the first mission to use short-wave radio for interstation contacts (1948).[58]

In 1947 Miss Lucille Jenkins of the Open Bible Standard Church, who had been with the Assemblies of God mission, began a separate mission at River Cess. This is more heavily involved in institutional work than most of the Assemblies of God missions. Manned by a staff of only two couples and three single women, there are a Bible school, a school, and a clinic.

---

[57] Letter to the author from Miss Katie Jean Jones, divisional secretary of the Assemblies of God in Liberia, June 24, 1964.

[58] Letter to the author from Ralph Hollondsworth, chairman, Liberian Field Fellowship, Assemblies of God, in response to Institute of Church Growth questions, April 11, 1965.

With only 200 full members in 14 villages in 1964, this mission has not had exceptional growth.[59]

Two other Pentecostal missions have experienced similar slow growth. The United Pentecostal Church has worked in Liberia since 1938. It now has two stations near Bomi Hills and one in the Belle tribe. The Pentecostal Assemblies of the World have one mission station in Liberia at Salala and a midwifery and child care clinic at Kakata.

These examples demonstrate that a Pentecostal theology is not sufficient to guarantee rapid growth. Nor is faithful mission work—no matter how good. A responsive people, a definite plan for planting churches, and a willingness to accept believers into membership are much more significant for the growth of the Church.

The most recent Pentecostal denomination to begin work in Liberia has met with greatest success; Swedish Pentecostals have major stations at Voinjama and at Foya Kamara near the Sierra Leone and Guinea borders in the northernmost corner of Liberia. They are located in roughly the same area as the Episcopal Order of the Holy Cross. From its beginnings in a revival in 1948, this Church has grown to 1,200 members in Liberia alone. There has been growth in both Guinea and Sierra Leone; but because of difficulties in ministering to converts across the border, churches in Sierra Leone have been turned over to the Assemblies of God based in Freetown, and churches in Guinea to the Christian and Missionary Alliance in that country. The best response has been in the Kissi tribe. There are churches in nearly every Kissi village—even the small ones—between Foya Kamara and the Guinea border.[60] This is the same tribe in which a sister working out of the Bolahun mission has had large baptism classes.[61] If, as this evidence seems to indicate, the Kissi tribe is the responsive unit in this area, all missions and Churches concerned should plant churches in every village and

[59] From an interview with the Rev. H. G. Hallberg, June 1964.
[60] From an interview with the Rev. Monro Paulson, June 1964.
[61] Smith interview.

make every effort to bring the Kissi to penitence and Christian faith while the response is favorable. Churches and missions working in the Kissi tribe need to study prayerfully the growing body of knowledge of people movements. Multi-individual conversion is an important key to church growth in this area. It is not sufficient to establish small churches of youth in rebellion against their elders, so that the tribe is arrayed against the Church. Instead, the tribe, the clan, and the family lineage should as far as possible be baptized into Christ—to be of service to the Church.

Evangelism in the very northern area takes on a critical significance because of the fact that this is one of the places in Liberia where Islam is both articulate and actively engaged in winning converts from among the pagan tribesmen.

In several ways the Pentecostal Churches are well equipped for the encounter with the primitive animistic religion of the tribal Liberians. It has been observed that while other Protestants, on more or less rational and doctrinal grounds, denounce belief in evil spirits and animistic practices as "superstitions," Pentecostal Christians think of themselves as being "in the midst of the turmoil of the world of magic, in order to fight evil spirits face to face, with *the* Spirit." Instead of demythologizing the Gospel to make it more acceptable, the Pentecostals in effect mythologize all life for their converts, bringing everything into the realm of the spirit world.[62] A part of Pentecostal worship services often takes the form of direct encounter with the world of demons. Christian leaders lay hands on the sick to heal them and speak directly to the evil spirits who are causing disease. Pentecostal Christians claim that theirs is the only Church which combats sorcery, enchantment, and witchcraft. It may be that the Pentecostals' emphasis on the life of the Spirit and acceptance of the spirit world identifies them with tribal Liberians. The spirit world, which is feared by the people because it cannot be controlled, is made subject to a greater

[62] In a letter to Dr. Donald A. McGavran from Key Yuasa, researcher for the United Presbyterian Church in São Paulo, Brazil, December 1964.

power, God's Spirit, in a realm and on a level the people understand.

THE PROPHET HARRIS

One of the most outstanding examples of church growth by a people movement in all Africa is that started by William Harris in the years 1913-15. It is worth exploring in some detail, in order to see the dynamics of this kind of movement actually at work. Though the group conversions took place in Ivory Coast and western Ghana, Harris was a Liberian, and his mission must be understood as a manifestation of the faith of the Church in Liberia. He was not sent by any Church or mission society, but as he walked from village to village in Ivory Coast, whole villages heard him and believed.

William Wade Harris was born of Grebo parents near Cape Palmas and the Ivory Coast border.[63] He attended mission schools and read books Bishop Auer had translated into Grebo; he also taught in the Protestant Episcopal schools from 1892 to 1909. For some time he lived with a Methodist colonist pastor in Cape Palmas, the Rev. Jesse Lawry. In 1909, without giving any reason, he raised the British flag, for which he was immediately imprisoned. On his release from jail, he began preaching in Ivory Coast, to the south.[64]

He was an arresting figure, tall, dressed simply yet impressively in a long white robe with a narrow red stole. He had a white beard and a mustache, and in a photograph taken of him in the Ivory Coast appears something over sixty years old.[65] He carried a well-worn Bible and a long bamboo staff with a short piece tied across it to form a cross; but if anyone mistook it for a fetish, he would break it before their eyes and throw it away and make another. He also carried a small gourd of

[63] Cyril J. Davey, *The March of Methodism* (New York: Philosophical Library, 1951), p. 156.

[64] Cason, *op. cit.*, p. 296.

[65] Raymond and Lu Verne Johnson, "Church Growth in the Ivory Coast" (Pasadena, Calif.: School of Missions, Fuller Theological Seminary, 1964), p. 12. Unpublished manuscript.

water. There were three women with him who helped to lead the singing.[66]

Harris had no earthly authority or commission, but believed that God had sent him forth. He spoke in pidgin English—which had to be translated by interpreters, for he did not know the languages of the people—and lived in simplicity, accepting his food and lodging from the villagers. He took no money except to give to the poor, and refused the extravagant gifts offered to him. In village after village his message was the same, simple and direct: "Repent and be baptized!" Converts were to burn their fetishes, observe Sunday, renounce alcohol, thieving, and adultery (neither Harris nor his followers were expected to give up polygamy).[67] They were to build churches and wait for white missionaries who would come and teach them how to obey God's Book. More than a hundred thousand persons turned from paganism.[68]

Twelve years after the movement began, when English Wesleyan missionaries learned of it, they found whole groups of villages where fetishism was dead. It had disappeared completely from the area in which Harris had preached. Its dances, cult feasts, charms, and symbols had been swept away and replaced by the Bible and an expectant waiting for those who would come to interpret it.

Harris' preaching is said to have been the result of a vow he made after an encounter with a leopard in the forest; and the legends about him say that angels spoke to him, and that a vulture brought him messages from the sky.[69] He himself asserted that the Angel Gabriel came to him and commissioned him to take the Gospel to those who had not heard.[70] Upon entering a village it was his practice to hold open-air services. If he was unknown there, he would begin by speaking to two or three whom he met, and soon a crowd would gather. He would

[66] Cason, *op. cit.*, p. 296.

[67] *Ibid.*

[68] Johnson and Johnson, *op. cit.*, p. 10.

[69] F. Deaville Walker, *The Story of the Ivory Coast* (London: Cargate Press, 1926), p. 13.

[70] Davey, *loc. cit.*

tell them of God. He proclaimed that there is one God and Savior, and all fetishes and idols are useless and must be destroyed. He would hold up his cross and God's Book and exhort the people to give up their wicked customs and live in honesty and righteousness. He appealed to them to become Christians, and invited those who would to be baptized then and there. The converts knelt on the ground, clasping the cross with both hands.

Then Harris laid his Bible on the convert's head and said, "This is God's Book. You must obey it. In the Name of the Father, the Son, and the Holy Spirit." Then he sprinkled water from a small calabash on the head of the convert. Sometimes groups of four or five would kneel at once and all grasp the long cross. He taught them to kneel and close their eyes to pray, but gave them no specific prayers. He exhorted them to show their new faith by changed lives. The new converts brought their fetishes and publicly burned them. Before he left, he admonished them to build a church, to keep the Sabbath by worshiping God, and to wait for the white man who would come with the Book.[71]

As noted, Harris represented no denomination, and never stayed in one village long enough to organize a church. He did advise the villagers, however, to appoint twelve apostles who would look after the collections and matters of business. These were all illiterate, and they continued at their work in the ordinary life of the village. Little bamboo and thatched churches sprang up in scores of villages where Harris had been.

He had more than he could do in just visiting the villages near the sea, yet he continually received pleas from villagers in the hinterland to come to them. He chose a few men and sent them to places where he could not go. Some of these prophets whom he appointed became influential men held in great esteem in the villages to which they were sent.

In 1914 Harris crossed the border into Gold Coast (now Ghana) and continued his preaching in the area known as Appolonia. In fifty-two villages fetishes were burned. About ten

---

[71] Johnson and Johnson, *op. cit.*, p. 15.

thousand Appolonians turned to God. At Harris' bidding, they sent requests for teachers to the Methodist missionaries in Axim. Thus in 1914 a Methodist Church was established in Appolonia, with many village congregations. After preaching there for about three months, Harris returned to the Ivory Coast.[72]

In 1915, with World War I going on in Europe, the French Government, fearing any sort of unrest that might lead to an uprising, decided to deport Harris. He was then preaching at Port Buoet near Abidjan, the capital. The administrator who was ordered to arrest him took along two soldiers and his cook boy. He found Harris on the surf-beaten beach, holding a service. Several people were kneeling on the sand praying. After the prayer Harris preached for ten or fifteen minutes, and the people sang a hymn, accompanied by stringed gourd rattles. Then the prophet called all those who desired baptism to come forward. As the administrator described it, there was perfect order, no excitement, no emotional outbreak. To his amazement, his own interpreter and cook boy came to him and asked permission to go forward with the others. The startled administrator nodded his consent, and the two knelt at the feet of the man they had come to arrest and received baptism at his hands.[73] At the close of the service the administrator carried out his instructions in the quietest way possible, requesting Harris to accompany him to the Liberian frontier. Harris submitted meekly without protest or opposition. He appealed to the people to make no trouble and to go home and serve the true God and not return to their fetishes. They stood silent, watching their beloved prophet walk quietly away with the administrator and his men. He was taken to the border of his native Liberia, 250 miles away, and warned not to return to French soil.[74]

Harris died years later, but his work remained after him despite considerable opposition.

[72] Arthur E. Southon, *Gold Coast Methodism* (London: Cargate Press, 1935), p. 47.
[73] Johnson and Johnson, *op. cit.*, p. 16.
[74] *Ibid.*

Having rid themselves of Harris, the [French] government decided to crush the movement he had started. The
administrator and inspector went from village to village in-
forming the people of the order and setting fire to the
bamboo and thatch churches. But the movement was not
easily destroyed. Eventually the people built stone and brick
churches and continued to worship as before. They had lost
their prophet; they had no one to teach them; they had no
shepherd, but Harris had told them that one day a white man
would come with the Book, and they settled down to wait his
coming. They were all illiterate and knew only the barest
facts of their new religion, but they were loyal to it and to
their prophet. Some of the groups managed to purchase bells,
and appointed bell-ringers to call the people to worship. They
had been taught to keep God's Day, and regardless of the
difficulty with their colonial employers, they kept it.

Assembling in God's house the people knelt in prayer. The
official "preacher," an unlearned man, would lead them. They
attempted singing snatches of the songs in pidgin English they
had managed to learn, though they understood nothing of it.
Sometimes their singing degenerated into mere humming, for
that was all they could remember. Sometimes someone broke
out in a song in their own language. The preacher would
repeat what they had heard Harris or one of his envoys
say.[75]

Fanti clerks from the Gold Coast came to work in some of
the villages near Abidjan in Ivory Coast. Many of them were
Methodists. Some, indeed, were local preachers or lay leaders.
These were the first to make contact with the "Harris Christians." In Ivory Coast, wherever they could, they strengthened
the new Christians by teaching them prayers and hymns and
helping them to obtain Bibles. The Bibles they bought were in
English, and when after that a Fanti lay preacher chanced to
pass through a village on Sunday, he could open up the Book
and read and exhort the people.

But in most churches, the Bible lay revered but unused as the
people waited for the promised missionaries. After the Sunday
service it was carefully wrapped in a cloth and put away until

[75] *Ibid.*

the following Sunday, when it was again displayed in its honored place on the altar. In 1923 an English Wesleyan Methodist pastor, the Rev. William J. Platt, on a trip to Abidjan met a lawyer who, on hearing he was a missionary, said, "Then what have you missionaries been doing for the last ten years? Away yonder there are thousands of village people waiting for you."[76] The lawyer told how a deputation of "Harris Christians" had come to his office with a bagful of money asking him to go to Europe and bring them missionaries. In the following year—1924—Mr. Platt made a trip visiting as many villages as he could. In every village he was welcomed with exuberant joy. Everywhere the cry was the same, "Send us teachers!" Platt made this amazing report when he got home to England. The English Missionary Society was in financial straits and had planned to curtail work in Ivory Coast, but on hearing Platt's report agreed to send three new missionaries. Though they were few, and it had been twelve years since some of the villagers had burned their fetishes, these missionaries gathered more than 45,000 into the churches from the people movement started by the prophet Harris.[77]

I have included this account of the people movement type of growth in the neighboring state of Ivory Coast because of its obvious implications for the expansion of the Church in Liberia. The same openness and receptivity that characterized the tribes in the coastal villages of Ivory Coast when Harris came to them in 1914 is evident in many Liberian villages of the interior today. The exact circumstances of the Harris movement cannot be repeated. But if some sort of people movement does take place, I wonder whether the Churches in Liberia will rise to the occasion. Indeed, in view of the general preoccupation of Churches and missions with large institutions and administrative organization, one wonders if the Churches in Liberia really want a people movement or will know how to shepherd the multitudes, once God moves the tribes of the hinterland.

[76] Walker, *op. cit.*, p. 32.
[77] Latourette, *A History of the Expansion of Christianity,* Vol. VII, *Advance Through the Storm* (New York: Harper & Brothers, 1945), p. 222.

CHAPTER V

ANTHROPOLOGY, A TOOL FOR CHURCH GROWTH

As we have seen, the Liberian people range from an educated elite to the illiterate tribal villagers. The Churches and
missions have so far been notably unsuccessful in evangelizing
the tribal population—because they have used methods of evangelism and patterns of church growth which are designed to
work in an already nominally Christian population, and because
the Church has been enclosed in the cultural prison of an
English-speaking community. The great social upheaval that is
changing Liberia has prepared tribal people for the Gospel.
Scattered pockets have already responded eagerly. This chapter
will describe the sociological process involved in group conversion. Conditions are favorable for the Church to grow by this
"new" process. Among the 900,000 tribal people, whole sections are ready to turn to Christ in movements that promise to
be amazing in both their proportions and their vitality.

The time is ripe for the Churches in Liberia to grow in
people-movement fashion. I use the correct term *people movement* here and throughout this volume to avoid the connotations
of *mass movement*, a term which conjures up visions of mass
hysteria or mass-produced mediocre Christianity. Bishop J.
Waskom Pickett in his amazing documentation of this type of
growth in India dispels all doubts as to the motives involved
and the vitality of the Christianity that results from genuine
people movements.[1]

I am convinced that group conversion and the people-
movement approach to evangelism are not only possible but
eminently suited for work among the Liberian tribes. More and
more missionaries and mission policy-makers are recognizing
that this is the best way for the Church to grow in non-

[1] J. Waskom Pickett, *Christian Mass Movements in India* (New
York: Abingdon Press, 1933).

123

Christian tribal populations such as these. The concept has been stated often and well—perhaps by no one more clearly than by A. L. Warnshuis, a knowledgeable mission theorist who was for many years co-secretary of the International Missionary Council. He writes:

> Briefly summarized, the wrong way to try to build up the Church in a non-Christian land is by the conversion of individuals extracted from dozens of different families, clans, villages and social groups. Such converts are promptly ostracized, separated from their relations and cut from their roots in the past of their own peoples. Such a church is only a conglomeration of individuals—often held together only by the cement of foreign money. That kind of church has no community interest nor any influence in the community and continues indefinitely dependent upon missionary aid.
>
> The better way is by recognition of the principle that the Church grows along racial lines in social strata. The right and natural growth of the Church is by the conversion of groups, where Christian forces help some group reconstruct its life, individual and corporate, around Jesus Christ.[2]

I am certain that the Holy Spirit is leading us in Liberia to choose the "better way."

PEOPLE MOVEMENT DEFINED

What the prophet Harris did was to start a typical people movement. It was exceedingly unfortunate that for ten years it was completely unshepherded. Yet even ten years after the original turning from idolatry, British Methodist missionaries found thousands of converts waiting to have the closed Bibles in their churches opened and explained to them. At this point missionaries working in Liberian village situations should ask themselves: if they were to leave a newly opened work without readers or preaching, what would be left of it ten years later?

Missions all around the world have grown in people-movement proportions. Perhaps the classic example of a people

[2] Pickett, Warnshuis, Singh, and McGavran, *Church Growth and Group Conversion* (Pasadena, Calif.: Fuller Theological Seminary, 1962), pp. 19-20.

movement took place among the Papuan tribesmen in New Guinea around the turn of the century, when whole tribes burned their fetishes and became Lutherans under the leadership and direction of missionary Christian Keyser.[3] The movement affected tribe after tribe, each moving into the Church guided by the mission that had worked in its area. Since the early Lutheran movements, other tribes have become Anglicans and Roman Catholics, and as recently as 1961 eight thousand members of the Dani tribe burned their fetishes in a single day, becoming Christians in the Christian and Missionary Alliance.[4]

A people movement of great proportions started in the Presbyterian Church in Pyongan Province, Korea, in 1897. It achieved greater momentum in 1907, at which time the Korean revival deepened the devotion of the existing churches and assisted in the further expansion of the movement. The Koreans are highly civilized compared to the aboriginal tribes of New Guinea. The pattern of growth was somewhat different, but the multitudes were the same.[5] Most people are familiar with the movements that have taken place in India, in which large parts of castes, often the lowly and oppressed classes, became Christians in a relatively short period of time.

Much of the growth of the Church that has taken place among the tribes in Liberia has been of the people-movement variety. But none of the movements has continued until a whole tribe or even a large part of it has been won to Christ. A people movement does not usually result in eight thousand converts in a single day. But large or small, it is the movement of a "people" or a part of a people. This term as used here means a homogeneous segment of the population. It may be a tribe or a caste, with common language and customs. It may be a smaller sociological unit—a clan or kinship grouping with a common

[3] G. F. Vicedom, *Church and People in New Guinea*, "World Christian Books," No. 38 (London: Lutterworth Press, 1961), p. 79.

[4] James Sunda, *Church Growth in West New Guinea* (Pasadena, Calif.: Fuller Theological Seminary, 1963), p. 27.

[5] Jonathan Goforth, *When the Spirit's Fire Swept Korea* (Grand Rapids, Mich.: Zondervan Publishing House, 1943), p. 37.

ancestor. For example, the Hebrews were a "people" in the society of the Egyptians before the Exodus, and the Jews of the Diaspora were a "people" in the larger context of the Gentile society of the Greco-Roman world. The "movement" takes place when small groups of persons within this society—sometimes ten, sometimes a hundred—decide together to become Christians.

Looked at anthropologically, the people movement is a process of culture change by which a group of mutually interdependent persons together make a decision to accept Christ as their Savior. The individual is the one who is saved, but he comes to Christ naturally within the framework of his society, together with some of his relatives and fellow tribesmen.[6]

Some readers are more accustomed to refer to expansion of the Church among the tribes as a "revival." But the term is not accurate, since the tribesmen involved are having their first encounter with Christ; there is nothing previously there to revive. A recapturing of vigor or renewal in an older established congregation is properly referred to as a revival, and such revival or renewal is a blessed event for the Christian community, but often does not lead to any larger movement toward Christ in a tribe or clan. Sometimes a revival results in almost no conversions from outside the Church at all. Hence, revival is not a good term to denote a movement toward Christ within a previously unevangelized people.

The questions immediately arise: What are the requisite conditions for successful people movements? Is there anything that can be done to encourage them? What can sustain a movement once it gets started? What steps may be taken to insure that the converts are really Christians and not merely baptized pagans? Is it really true that *acceptance* of Christ may rightly come before an educated understanding or spiritual growth? In an uneducated tribal person, in unity with his own family and group, can the *initial* conviction that Jesus is Lord form a sound basis for genuine Christian development? Can it be truly said

---

[6] McGavran, *Bridges of God,* Chaps. III and VI, has the definitive discussion of the "people movement."

that this is better than one-by-one conversion away from the tribe?

What can we do to start a people movement? Strictly speaking, this is beyond our powers. Surely, as Christians, we confess that "it is the Holy Spirit who calls, gathers, enlightens and sanctifies the whole Christian Church in the world."[7] This quotation from Luther's *Small Catechism* is memorized by every child in Lutheran confirmation classes, and all Christians have more or less similar confessions. God's Spirit is free and moves where and when He wills. He is the One who starts people movements.

The most important thing we can do is to pray that God, who is impatient for the return of His sons, will send His Holy Spirit upon us and upon the people who are yet in darkness. This is God's best gift, which our Lord promised we would receive if we would ask.[8] The gift of the Holy Spirit makes us a new creation in Christ, and this gift gives us the power to overcome our own sin and our own self-righteousness, and to do God's will.

We are also given the power to discern where the Spirit is leading us. For the Church to grow with the Spirit, missionaries and pastors must discern where the Spirit is leading. A functioning knowledge of the culture of the people, tribe, or clan whom we hope to bring to Christ is invaluable. Anthropology can provide this knowledge and help us to discern where the Holy Spirit is moving. We must not say that with the help of anthropology we can predict the movement of God's Holy Spirit. He is a free agent, moving where and when He wills; but He is just as able to help us discern His movements through the insights gained by the study of anthropology as to have us see a vision of a man saying, "Come over into Macedonia and help us."

Still less may we imagine that the patterns of human behavior compel the Holy Spirit in any way. He is sovereign and does what he pleases. But God is usually pleased to act in regular ways. Regular ways belong to God no less than ways for which

[7] Martin Luther, *Small Catechism*.
[8] Luke 11:13.

we find no explanation. The social laws discovered by anthropology and sociology are the ways God frequently uses. When we see a people become ready for change and open to acceptance of the Gospel, by faith we can discern the beneficent action of the Holy Spirit.

Every pastor knows the value of preaching to his audience. A preacher who uses the illustration of a train, for example, in preaching to people who have never seen a train will have a hard time making his point. For missionaries and boards doing work in Liberia it is vitally necessary that they know as much about the people among whom they work as possible, in order to make their point. Actually, very little research about the way tribesmen think or act has been or is being carried out by missions in Liberia. Most missionaries working there—even now—still cannot speak the language of the tribe among whom they work. Hardly any can accurately describe the kinship patterns of the people around them. Those working in urban-industrial centers of Westernized population may be at an even greater disadvantage. The people all speak English, and this may effectively conceal from the missionary the fact that his audience is not just like the folks back home. Knowledge of the cultural and social forces in men's lives should affect not only the kind of sermon preached but the missionary's every action.

CULTURE CHANGE AND CONVERSION

The study of anthropology has already been widely accepted among missionaries as a way to understand better the people they serve. But anthropology offers insights into the culture that have an even more direct bearing on the growth of the Church. The change that takes place in the individual when he is converted, and the change that takes place in society when enough individuals are converted, may be seen from the strictly scientific point of view as examples of culture change. The missionary, according to the anthropologist's definition, is the advocate or agent of culture change. The first villager converted is the innovator. The several changes in his life that take place because he is a new creation in Christ are innovations in behavior patterns.[9]

If enough members of the tribe or group change their behavior patterns, the old ways are no longer considered right, and new ways take their place. New cultural institutions are substituted for the old. Indeed, a time may come when the old ways are as abhorrent to the average member of the society or tribe as the new ways were when first introduced. The more Christians there are in a society, the more likely it is that the mores and practices of the society will change so as to become acceptable to Christians. This by no means makes every member of the society a Christian. But it does make it possible and even probable that every member will at least hear the Gospel sympathetically and have the opportunity, as an individual, to decide to follow Christ. At the same time, the groups of Christians work together to bring the structure of society into conformity with Christian principles.

Surely we all recognize that there is a tremendous difference between the kind of change that takes place when a group stops using clay waterpots and starts using tin buckets and the change involved when a group renounces chicken-sacrificing animism and adheres to churchgoing, Bible-reading Christianity. One involves drawing water for cooking. The other involves the water of life. But, anthropologically speaking, the changes have similarities that can be compared. By looking at conversion as an example of culture change, it is possible for the missionary to gain new insights into the process and to discern better the leading of the Holy Spirit.

The subject of culture change is a science in its own right, and it is impossible here to present even the barest outline of the anthropology involved. But some of the insights of anthropology have such exciting implications for the growth of the Church that they must be shared here.[10]

[9] Louis J. Luzbetak, *The Church and the Cultures* (Techny, Ill.: Divine Word Publications, 1963), p. 5.

[10] A definitive work on the subject of culture change which has insights for the student of mission church growth is H. G. Barnett, *Innovation: The Basis of Culture Change* (New York: McGraw-Hill Book Company, 1953), p. 462.

THE HOMOGENEOUS UNIT

Society is not an amorphous mass. It is made up of separate, even isolated, groups of people which, following McGavran, I shall refer to as homogeneous units. The units are homogeneous because they have important culture traits in common that separate them from other homogeneous units in the society. Language, for example, is one of the most important distinguishing traits, and even the casual observer recognizes that the sixteen tribes in Liberia have sixteen different languages and are therefore sixteen homogeneous units. In many tribal areas the preacher and the missionary who speak nothing but English communicate only with the small segment of the population that really understands English. Their message is subject to the constant imprecision and error of interpreters. In addition to a common language, each tribe has common customs and social institutions—religious beliefs and practices which its members may consider more significant even than their language. It is important, therefore, that the preacher recognize the tribe and take it seriously.

That the tribe is a homogeneous unit is obvious. Multiple subgroupings are not so obvious, but are often more significant for church growth. These smaller groupings are even more homogeneous than the tribe—that is, the members have closer ties and more attributes in common. Some of these unifying traits may be based on location, e.g., a village, or a "quarter" in a village. Some of the divisions are based on kinship, such as extended family or clan. In some cases economic circumstances such as poverty or dependence on a particular occupation are the unifying factors. More often several of these elements in combination unite the group.

Each homogeneous unit has a strong people consciousness. When a man considers becoming a Christian he always thinks of the effect it will have on his tribal relationships, his kinsmen, and his way of life. Some groupings are effectively hidden from the missionary because there is nothing corresponding to them in his own culture. The ties of clan or extended family are likely to seem unnecessarily complex or foolishly arbitrary to the uninitiated Westerner. But for evangelism they may be the most significant of all. It is impossible to guess about these relationships. They must be discovered from actual case studies. Interviews that are simple and direct, in which questions can be answered objectively, may give a missionary a tremendous advantage in approaching a homogeneous unit with the Gospel.[11]

Bearing on Church Growth. The homogeneous units in society have important bearing on the spontaneous and rapid expansion of the Church: first, because when the Gospel moves from person to person it moves most rapidly and easily within the framework of the society—that is, within these units. The ties between members of homogeneous units are what Dr. McGavran calls "bridges of God." Across them the message of the Gospel may be easily communicated. One cannot generalize about the kind of contacts most important to the transmission of the Gospel. In one tribe the extended family relationships may be very strong and constitute an effective vehicle. In another, the geographical layout of the village may prove most important. All contacts are useful, of course, but in any given situation, discovering which relationships are most vital may make the difference between a vigorous, continuing people movement and an arrested, sickly movement—or, as is often the case, no movement at all.

Second, these homogeneous units are important to church growth because the individuals within them share many traits in common, including their basic ideas and general outlook. When a member of a group is miraculously healed at a mission hospital, the whole group knows about it and shares the experience. The general attitude of the group is formed in the same mold. When the attitude toward the Gospel changes from hostility to friendliness, the whole group feels satisfied about becoming Christian.

This operative group atmosphere exists in all societies. In the average American town, for example, there is a generally favor-

---

[11] The author discovered the importance of extended family ties for evangelism among the Loma by asking more than a hundred converts the question, "Who was the person who first spoke to you about becoming a Christian?" "What is his relationship to you?"

able attitude toward joining a church but a very strong antipathy toward joining the Communist Party. One might go from door to door inviting people to join a church and expect some affirmative response; but a similar canvass to promote the Communist Party would be likely to meet with a violent negative response. Among the homogeneous units of Liberian society, reactions to the Gospel run the whole gamut. When members are resistant to the thought of exchanging their old ways for a new life in Christ, the task in evangelism may rightly be compared with the sowing of seed, or even with plowing rocky soil. But when a homogeneous unit is open and receptive to the idea of change, it is ripe for harvest. Seed-sowing evangelistic methods must be replaced by those that reap, that bring in the harvest. To know as much as possible about the group attitudes of the homogeneous unit is essential.

Third and most important of all, these units act as a group and *can decide together* to become Christians. Anthropology has demonstrated that in societies like the tribes of Liberia, culture change normally does *not* take place in one individual at a time until the whole society is affected, but that groups within the society can and do adopt these changes *as groups*. This concept of the homogeneous unit and group conversion has most exciting applications to evangelism and church growth.

Each individual in a group contributes to the decision. It is hardly ever the case that the leader decides and all the rest follow unthinkingly, like sheep. Neither is it exactly a matter of majority rule. According to the customs of the group, the judgment of certain important individuals (wise old leaders, for example) is given relatively more weight than that of the younger men, or women and children. Members of the society look for a reliable guide to action in family, clan, or class relationships.

In some societies "decisions which purport to be group decisions must in fact be considered individual decisions, but a representative makes the decision."[12] In such cases the decision of a single chief to become a Christian may have a greater effect

[12] Raymond Firth, ed., *Man and Culture* (London: Routledge & Kegan Paul, 1957), pp. 38-40.

on community practice than that of a dozen young men, but no chief is likely to decide all by himself. He feels out his followers first.

The young men in a group may be free to become Christians individually in spite in the group feeling—in fact, almost in reaction against the old authority. But when this happens church growth is painfully slow, for the converts include only those who are strong enough to revolt against the established order, or who are different from other members of the society— prophets or misfits. The schoolboy converts in so many missions in Liberia are a good example of this kind of growth. But if the young men's old grandfather—who is closest to the ancestors (after all, he has known more of them personally than anyone else still living!)—if such a man decides that it is a good thing to follow Christ, the whole kinship group may follow him into the Church.

It must not be imagined that individual members of the group do not become good Christians merely because they join the Church as a group. If anything, just the opposite is true. Those who are converted as individuals in violation of the will of the group are much more likely to backslide than those who come to Christ with their society intact.[13] These homogeneous units function in every society, and they affect the growth of Churches in Europe and America, though the units are often smaller and the individual has relatively more freedom of action than in tribal societies.

For example, I am a Christian—a new creation by God's grace. I was a small child when my parents started taking me to church. It may be argued that I am a Christian because my family was Christian, and that my faith is not my own but the product of my culture, my family, and my Church. All this may be so, but I am not ashamed of my Christian family. On the contrary, I am thankful to God for it, and am no less a Christian because of being taken to church as a child than the man who was converted alone, as an adult, out of an American pagan family. If the homogeneous unit functions for an American in a society that almost idolizes the individual and his

[13] Pickett, *op. cit.*, p. 331.

decisions, how much more important it is for the tribal Liberian whose whole society is oriented to obedience within a larger group!

These group divisions—the tribe, the clan, and the extended family—are powerful forces in the culture of Liberian tribes, with strong claims on the lives of the members. Much is said about the passing of tribal society in Africa. It is true that the tight control of the tribes is weakening, but missionaries would do well not to underestimate the old social order as a current force in the lives of the people—even for those who, by all outward appearance, are rejecting the old order in favor of Western ways. It is always difficult for a missionary to make converts one by one where the tribal society is strong. Some of the individuals he approaches would be willing to become Christians, but they remain outside the Church because of the pressures of the resistant group. This has led some missionaries and Christian leaders to identify the tribe and the existing social order as enemies of the Gospel. This is as false as saying that the family is the enemy of the Gospel in America. Some families, it is true, bring pressure on their members not to become Christians, but there are just as many who help their individual members to grow in grace and remain strong in the faith. The family unit is neither Christian nor anti-Christian of itself.

The family is a social unit that must be taken into consideration, and should be preserved because it helps the individual. The same thing must be said of the larger homogeneous units in a tribal society. The inertia of tribal loyalties, which keeps members of the tribe from becoming Christians when Christianity is a strange new faith, can become a powerful force impelling individuals to decide for Christ, a landslide sweeping the whole group into the Church when once a movement begins. In this era of rapid social change, when so many tribesmen in Liberia are moving to the cities and industrial centers and are becoming so much less conscious of their tribal identity, some feel that all church growth considerations relating to these homogeneous units of society must be abandoned. This view has little basis in sound fact. The actual pattern of church expansion in

Liberia, where it is now taking place, supports the homogeneous unit thesis. The best way to evangelize the displaced tribal wage earners is to start a people movement in their upcountry village.

TWO CONVERSIONS

For some church leaders this concept of group conversion may be more palatable if we describe it in terms of two conversions as recounted by James Sunda in his book, *Church Growth in West New Guinea*.[14] When the eight thousand Dani tribesmen burned their fetishes and began to take regular Christian instruction, that was a "conversion *out of paganism*." A few months later, individual persons who had been instructed and had confessed Christ were baptized in groups of from ten to a hundred—this was their conversion *into Christianity*. Many denominations in Liberia already provide for such a sequence of decisions. The Loma converts in my own parish *lo Gala gaazu* (literally, "stand before God's face") in a service one Sunday, and become members of the baptism instruction class. Four months or so later they are received into membership by baptism.

The average pastor in the United States understands the family patterns of the members of his congregation, because he grew up in that culture and is familiar with it. For the Church in Liberia to grow at its full potential, missionaries and pastors must learn the important relationships between members in the tribal society. Properly understood and evangelized, there is no reason why the homogeneous units of a tribal society cannot receive Christ just as the jailer at Philippi who was baptized "and all who were in his house."[15]

Our problem is twofold. First, we must recognize the unit that can function like the household of the Philippian jailer. It may be the family, or it might possibly be a larger unit: a clan or village, a town or a quarter. It is obvious that a family can become Christians together as did that of the Philippian jailer. But it is not so obvious what constitutes a family. The biologi-

14 Sunda, *op. cit.*
15 Acts 17:34.

cal relationships included in the immediate family differ from one society to another. If the Philippian jailer had been a Loma tribesman, his household would have included a much larger extended family. The Holy Spirit prepares a segment of a population to respond to the Gospel. Our task is to use every means in our power to understand what the largest unit of society is that can consider Christianity, and to help its members as a whole to choose Christ. If the group accepting Christ is larger than the household of the Philippian jailer, then let us instruct its members most carefully, baptize them, and rejoice in the Spirit of God who works such conversions.

Second, our problem is that we must learn how to approach the group so that the whole unit can respond as a unit. In the case of the jailer, Paul converted the head of the household, and automatically the whole household became Christians. Had he converted only one of the sons, the father might have taken offense at his son making such an important decision without consulting him, might have reacted violently—might even have become an enemy of the Gospel.

There are modes of approach to tribesmen which show due respect to the chiefs and to the elders of the village or clan. There are suitable ways to approach their conversion as a whole unit that will not offend the tribal sense of propriety. Using these, the very least we can hope for is that the old men will not stand in the way of those within the group who do want to become Christians. They may even lead them. If missionaries pray for group conversions and expect them, God may grant that the whole group—slowly, with the same deliberation with which they would decide to move their village to a new site—will decide that Christ is the hope of their lives, individually and collectively.

I am not here advocating a new way of conversion. It is at least as old as St. Peter's approach to Cornelius or St. Paul's to the synagogue community at Berea, [16] and has its roots even earlier in experiences of the people of God recounted in the Old Testament. But people movements have not been widely accepted by missionaries and church leaders because they are so

[16] Acts 10 and 27.

different from the European and American pattern of individual accessions to the Church, which they have been taught, and have come to accept, as a norm and as the only way for the Church to grow.

Our Lord compared making disciples to harvesting a crop. The methods of evangelism, like harvest methods, are different from place to place. The Loma woman harvests the rice on her small farm using a knife with a blade about two inches long. She cuts the rice one stalk at a time, as an American housewife might cut flowers. When she has a handful of heads, as we saw earlier, she ties them in a bundle with a rice straw. This is slow work. In the field where she labors, with stumps sticking up and logs lying helter-skelter, mechanized equipment could not move. What a contrast this kind of harvest is to what takes place in the thousand-acre wheat fields of the American Midwest, where grain is harvested by huge, self-propelled combines. A Kansas farmer would not even look at the Loma woman's knife, much less try to use it. He would need a thousand wives! And a combine would be equally useless in a Liberian rice field, since it could not make its way among the stumps and logs. The methods used for harvest must be workable in each particular field.

The fields for harvest in evangelism in America and in tribal Liberia are just as different as their grain fields. In the United States 50 per cent of the population claim at least some connection with the Church, and even unbelievers are greatly influenced by the Christian outlook. In such a society, individuals are approached because they can be expected to make individual decisions to join the Church. In some parts of Liberia this pattern is workable. But in the tribal areas, where the extended family and the tribe are still strong social factors (and solidly pagan), it is not possible to win a whole nation by Western individualistic methods—trying to persuade individuals, in defiance of their social instincts, to renounce their tribe for Christianity. Winning one at a time in our Western way is as wasteful of time and energy there (and often actually obstructive in effect) as to go into a ripe Kansas wheat field with a paring knife. The Kansas farmer would not be patient with hired hands who went to harvest thus equipped. The harvest is just too great. Whole fields are ready, and our Western paring-knife methods are not sufficient for the task. People movements are.

INSTITUTIONS REPLACE INSTITUTIONS

Another insight from the discipline of anthropology which has significance for the growth of the Church is the concept that culture changes take place completely only when whole institutions of a society are replaced by other institutions. This is taking the word, of course, in a broader sense than that of a school, college, or hospital. As used here "institution" refers to a fairly permanent complex, an integrated pattern of behavior by which social control is exerted among human beings. Thus there is the institution of marriage, the institution of barter and trade, and so on.[17]

Culture change can take place at several levels. Individual items or traits in a society may change. For example, the natural dye used to color cotton thread for weaving may be replaced by commercial dye. At another level whole groups of such culture traits can change; thus in the culture complex of weaving, every item may be replaced and a complete new method adopted. Or on a yet higher level, whole institutions in society may change so that a man gives up weaving cloth altogether, becomes a wage earner in a money economy, and buys his clothes ready-made. In every society, culture changes take place continuously on many levels. The introduction of Christianity involves changes at all three levels just mentioned, but it is important for Christian leaders to realize that in seeking to plant the Church in Africa they are not primarily concerned with changes at a superficial level. They are introducing a whole institution (the Church) into the culture. In the process, it will replace certain institutions (ancestor worship) and change others (marriage, polygamy). The task is made more difficult because an important institution such as ancestor worship or polygamy

[17] Charles Winick, *Dictionary of Anthropology* (Paterson, N. J.: Littlefield, Adams & Co., 1961), p. 287.

has its roots in all aspects of the culture. And old institutions are tenacious.

> A comprehensive institution endures because it is organically connected and satisfies an essential need of society. It can be suppressed, but is then driven underground. It can be mutilated, deprived of this or that aspect or prerogative, but it disappears only with the destruction of the whole cultural identity of a people. Either this, or else it *can be replaced by a more adequate institution,* fulfilling the same function, satisfying the same needs, and conforming, let us say, to the standards of western civilization (italics mine).[18]

The Church must be the "more adequate institution," which fulfills the functions and satisfies the needs of the society so well that the old institutions are abandoned as insufficient.

First of all, it must be recognized that the African Church cannot be merely an institution of Western culture, transplanted from America or Europe but with Africans in the pulpit and pews. Neither will it be simply an institution of the old Africa with a few modifications. The new institution will not be a mixture of both cultures. Dr. H. G. Barnett says that the new "configuration," as he calls it, is like an offspring of the institutions in the two parent cultures—resembling both parents, but completely different, a new integrated whole.[19] The Church in Africa will be that kind of new institution, an African Church. The functions the African Church assumes in society, and the way it meets the felt needs of the people, will greatly affect both the rate and extent of its growth.

When in a culture change one institution (the Church) replaces another (ancestor worship) in the life of the people, every function of the former must be replaced. If the process is not complete, there will be a vacuum in the new situation which will undercut its effectiveness. The functions that are not taken over by the Church will remain under the influence of the old religion, and will become a reservoir to preserve it, and a breeding place of resistance to Christianity.[20]

---

[18] Bronislaw Malinowski, *Dynamics of Culture Change* (New Haven: Yale University Press, 1945), p. 53.

[19] Barnett, *op. cit.*, p. 181.

[20] Malinowski, *loc. cit.*

Sometimes the Church fails to grow because it fulfills only a part of the functions of the old institution. Sometimes it is not accepted because it does not meet the felt needs of the people. Missionaries and African Church leaders must discover and meet these needs. For example, blood sacrifice is a feature of the old religious institutions which is universally rejected by Christians on the theological grounds that Christ's sacrifice on the cross is sufficient for all our needs. The principle we are considering means that if the Church is effectively to replace the old institution and fulfill its functions, it must meet the needs that were formerly met by blood sacrifice—but in a new way. The tribal men in Liberia celebrate ritual sacrifices before starting to "make a farm." The dangers implicit in the slash-and-burn method and the possibilities of crop failure in this kind of farming give a man every reason to seek help and guidance at this time. Yet I found only one mission that reported special rogation or seedtime services.

On the other hand, every mission stresses Christian marriage ceremonies with special church services. But in the Loma tribe, at least, marriage is strictly a social agreement, a bargain between two family units. It is not a religious festival at all, and no sacrifices are made for it. In other words, most congregations in the tribal areas have failed to function as the old institution did in meeting the felt need of preparation for planting; while, on the other hand, they are carrying over the function of the marriage ceremony, which meets the felt needs of another society: viz., America. The new African Church must have both—a rogation service to meet the age-old need at seedtime, and a religious marriage ceremony to meet the needs of the new monogamous society that is emerging. In this way it will not only do what the old institutions did, but will meet new needs which the old institutions did not meet. It will then be *a more adequate institution.*[21]

In the present situation converts feel the need for special help when the farm season approaches, but since the Church offers no rogation services they are tempted to go along with their non-Christian neighbors and make the old sacrifices. Thus the

[21] *Ibid.*

old institution still has a foothold in the society because it still fulfills a legitimate function that meets the felt needs of the people. In the one mission that does have a rogation service, the farmers bring their tools to each little church, and a service is held in which special prayers are made for protection during the farming season and for a bountiful harvest. Here the Church is faithfully meeting the felt need of the people.

Identification of function and felt need is very important for the African Church, if it is to replace the old institutions. For example, one would have expected the bush schools, *poro* and *sande,* to disappear after the thousands of dollars and years of service that have been invested in mission and public schools; especially in an area like the Zorzor district, where in a pilot project a large number of public schools have been erected by the government. Yet the bush school is still strong, and school-boys, even college graduates, enter it. We must not be misled by the term "school" and expect mission schools to replace bush schools. The two are not equivalent. The bush school has other functions, and is evidently meeting felt needs of the people which the mission or public school does not. Thus it continues to exist side by side with the new institution.

What are these functions? Does the Church have a substitute, so that it can replace the old religion in this matter? Or can the Church take over the bush school? Surely it is not impossible for such a pattern of initiation to be taken over by the Church, with adjustments, so that the practices abhorrent to Christians, such as clitoridectomy, female circumcision, scarification, sacrifice, and the like, would be abandoned. The time these children and youth spend in the tribal initiation bush school would be a ready-made opportunity for Bible study and Christian instruction bearing on coming of age, Christian sex attitudes, and other aspects of mature Christian life.

For the Church to grow, it is of utmost importance that the prospective convert recognize it as an alternative institution *fulfilling* the same functions and meeting the same felt needs as the old one. One reason the Church has grown so slowly in tribal Liberia is that the Christianity there presented has been so completely different from anything the tribal people recognize as a religious experience that they fail to identify the Church as an alternative to their old religious institutions. A missionary or a Liberian pastor would be wise not to mock the cult religion, but to study it, and not clothe Christianity in trappings (literacy, Western clothes, Western social mores) so different from what the tribal man knows as religion that he is unable to recognize it as religion at all.[22]

By this very element of identification, Islam is making inroads into the animistic tribes of West Africa. A Muslim trader will settle in a village and live with the people. His religion would not be recognized by orthodox Muslims as Islam at all, but he does kneel down in the morning and face Mecca to pray. He tells fortunes and becomes one among several persons whom the villagers will seek out in time of need, sickness, or misfortune, or before making sacrifices at farm time. His name for God is accepted as an alternative form along with the villagers' own name for God. By the time there are ten Muslims in the village, there will be one boy who has learned to write a few holy verses. When there are twenty men, they will build a mosque. When the pagans start bringing their sons to the Muslim leader for a naming ceremony, the whole village is on its way to becoming Muslim. Parrinder says somewhere that when a man stops praying to his ancestors and starts praying to Allah for them, he is a Muslim. But I would say that men are predisposed to accept Islam a long time before they reach that stage.

The people of Liberia's tribes are, in fact, predisposed toward becoming Christians. Their President and the elite are Christians; their own educated sons and daughters are Christians. The Church of Jesus Christ can meet their felt needs, but it is not enough for the missionaries to identify these needs and offer a well-intended solution for them. The people themselves must recognize the functions the Church assumes as a fulfillment of their need. When this happens, they will abandon the weak old institutions and cling to the adequate one: the Church of Jesus Christ.

[22] Luzbetak, *op. cit.*, p. 96. A definition of "identification and empathy" is given.

CHAPTER VI

BARRIERS AT THE CHURCH DOOR

CHURCHES MUST BE WILLING

Two things are necessary for a people movement toward Christ to take place. It is not enough that the people be ready to move. It is just as important that the Church be willing to receive them. When a homogeneous unit in society is ready to change, its members are receptive to the idea of exchanging their old institutions for a new one. The eye of faith recognizes that the Holy Spirit has prepared them and brought them to this moment of decision. But for this ripe field to be harvested for Christ, the Church must be ready and willing to make disciples of them. It is false to assume that all missions and all Churches desire the discipling of the nations (or tribes), or are ready to receive them.

For example, in West New Guinea when eight thousand Dani tribesmen burned their fetishes and prepared to become Christians in the Christian and Missionary Alliance, there were missions in the same area which refused to have anything to do with the fetish burnings. The story is told that when a large group showed up at one mission station to burn fetishes, the missionary in charge, shotgun in hand, actually drove them away. The encounter between the Churches in Liberia and a "people" ripe for harvest is not likely to be quite so dramatic, but it is just as possible for Churches and missionaries to turn their backs on opportunities for people-movement expansion.

There are four ecclesiological factors most likely to cause missionaries and pastors to miss the opportunities for church growth that exist. First, they do not understand church growth by people movements; second, they already have systems that produce little growth; third, they do not expect church growth; and fourth, they are not willing to make sacrifices for it. Many churchmen—it is a surprising thing, really—do not understand the rapid expansion of the Church. I asked more than forty church leaders and missionaries in Liberia the question, "To what do you attribute the slow growth of your Church?" Their replies fall into two categories, of which the first was: "We are working with a very difficult situation. Men are unresponsive, and do not want to leave paganism. The church necessarily grows slowly."[1] In some areas this explanation may be valid, but where another denomination is making converts rapidly in the same homogeneous unit, it is obviously untrue.

Men of the second group blame their theology. "We preach only the true biblical doctrine. One cannot expect large numbers of people to accept the truth." This has the ring of denominational pride. But investigation shows that denominational doctrines, except in rare instances, are not the real explanation. The same denomination has had growth of the people-movement type in other countries of the world. And the very same explanation is given by some missionaries who have experienced notable growth—but with a suitably different conclusion. They say, "We preach the true biblical doctrine, and therefore God has blessed our preaching with great growth." Ah me!

After I received versions of this second answer from five missionaries representing five denominations with greatly divergent theological positions, I began to suspect that the "theological" explanation of growth or lack of it was too simple and, in fact, concealed more than it revealed. The truth is that people-movement growth around the world has not been limited to any one denomination, or even one family of denominations with a common theological position. As long as churchmen give prideful theological excuses for little growth, they will not discern the real reasons, and may indeed continue to use the same faulty methods with the same disappointing results.

No Christian should be satisfied with a simple explanation that justifies defeat until he has exhaustively examined every aspect of the culture and the situation for some clue to the real reasons for slow growth.

Theological Positions That Discourage Growth. It must be admitted, however, that some theological positions are a hindrance to the growth of the church. Some conservative positions become very legalistic. Missionaries holding these views are in danger of finding themselves like the scribes and Pharisees of

---

[1] See Appendix A for a list of persons interviewed.

whom Jesus said that they would cross sea and land to make a single proselyte, and make him twice as much a child of hell as themselves. Other missionaries—like the circumcision party— demand conduct of new converts that is based on law and not grace. Legalism is by no means limited to any one denomination, but wherever it occurs, it blocks the channels of God's grace and stops church growth.

The Churches must serve as avenues of God's grace through which He reaches out to the unsaved millions. If these channels become blocked by legalism, then the flow of grace will be hindered, but God will not let it be stopped entirely. If we are too leisurely in discipling the tribes and nations, or if we are stingy with God's grace, He will not be content with us and will break out of our channel. The Holy Spirit is able to go past us and use someone else to reach the people, even if it has to be someone whose theology is not as sharply focused as we think ours is. He may use what we call sects or even cults to accomplish His purpose, and then take a generation or more to perfect them. The end result will be a people who worship Him in truth, and God will accept their praise whether they are called Lutheran, Baptist, Roman Catholic, or Pentecostal.

The growth of the Holy Ghost cult in Lutheran territory in Liberia is a sign that, rapid as the Lutheran growth was, it was too slow in reaching out to shepherd the people movement then (and perhaps still) under way in the Totota area. At the other end of the spectrum, some missionaries and denominations are so liberal they have no real concern to communicate the Gospel of salvation. They do not care if their Church grows or not; and it does not. These theological positions to the far left and right may be truly responsible here and there for lack of church growth. But between the two extremes there are many theological positions that do make room for growth to take place.[2]

---

[2] A mimeographed sheet of eight "Distinctive Baptist Principles" enumerated by one of the most conservative groups in Liberia, the Mid-Liberian Baptist Mission, has nothing in it that would necessarily preclude a church-growth point of view. Secondary interpolations of the eight distinctions and strong emphasis on the word "individual," where it occurs in three of the distinctive principles, might make a people movement unlikely.

GOD'S IMPATIENCE IN LIBERIA

Biblical evidence shows that God often deals with men in families, including actual examples of the rapid expansion of the New Testament Church by group conversion. "God sets the solitary in families," and unbelieving husbands and wives are sanctified by their believing mate.[3] All through the book of Acts are reports of multitudes who come to Christ.[4]

On Pentecost the baptism of three thousand in a single day resembled nothing so much as a people movement. Pentecost was more like the conversion of the Dani tribe in New Guinea than any church growth that is taking place in Liberia today. Those who object to the emphasis on numbers should remember that, if he had not counted the sheep, the shepherd would not have known that one was lost.[5]

In Liberia it is the ninety-nine of the tribal people who are lost, and if churchmen keep in mind God's will that men be saved, and remember the multitudes of the unsaved, they will not be content with evangelistic methods that reap no harvest, or too easily alarmed or offended to try other ways.

Theology for Church Growth in Africa. While the theological positions of most Churches make church growth possible, there is little in these theologies that actually *promotes* the rapid growth of the Church in the African situation. To begin with, the position of the Liberian Churches is largely defined by that of the sending Churches. These theologies have been hammered out on the anvil of controversy between opposing factions in Christendom. Reformation theology was formed in a debate with Roman Catholicism of the sixteenth century. Revival theology has been formulated over against the antirevivalists. Even denominations that claim no creed but the Bible explain their various interpretations of it as against positions taken by other Christians. When an American missionary uses as biblical a term such as "new birth" he is thinking of what happened to him back home in Indiana where he grew up in a Christian family and went to Sunday school. His experience is not necessarily normative for a tribesman in an African village.

[3] I Cor. 7:14.
[4] Acts 5:14, 8:6, 13:45.
[5] Acts 2:41, Luke 15:4.

The theologies developed in the West are of little help to the African Church in its encounter with the pagan society by which it is surrounded. Contemporary Western theologians, for example, are writing about renewal and revival in the "Christian" societies of the West. In those societies, expansion of the Church by a people-movement pattern is quite impossible and never comes in question. Naturally their theologies have nothing to say about this kind of evangelism. But the African Church faces a close-knit tribal society in which the masses of the people have not yet had their first encounter with Christ. This Church needs a theology that will take the ninety-and-nine lost sheep of the pagan masses seriously—a theology of evangelism that will be pleasing to God, who demands obedience in proportion to the potential for church growth.[6]

THE INDEFINITELY REPRODUCIBLE PATTERN

For the established Churches, the greatest roadblock to rapid expansion is that they already have existing patterns, and these are patterns that produce little growth. This is especially true in the tribal areas of Liberia. The existing pattern there is based on the central mission-station approach, in which hospital, school, and church are all part of the "mission work." In this pattern, the Church grows slowly through one-by-one accessions from among the schoolboys who speak English, and later from among their wives and families. Preachers are hired by the missions, with salaries subsidized from mission funds. Church buildings are constructed of concrete or bricks in a Western style of architecture. This old pattern still dominates mission work today. The missionaries supervise the system and contribute their effort to making it work. What the tribal man learns from this is that the way a person becomes a Christian is by fitting into the system—that is, going to the mission school, or working for the missionary, or adopting the values and standards of the system. National pastors are often more bound by the system than the missionaries. They have come up through it and know it from the inside, so to speak.

[6] McGavran, *How Churches Grow,* pp. 1-9.

The whole pattern of missions is affected by this system. Evangelism and growth of the Church take place at a rate entirely governed by it. No one expects the rate of church growth to exceed a certain percentage (depending on the number of students going through the school, plus a small number of other persons who for one reason or another are willing to fit in). This is the way the system works.

We must no longer be patiently bound by this system. Under our circumstances, patience is no virtue. The time has come for the African Church to cast off its mission-station fetters and develop a pattern of church growth that will better meet the opportunities. In proposing such a pattern for today's situation, I do not at all intend to belittle the great missionaries and church leaders who have gone before. The numerous martyrs among them are sufficient evidence of their courage and dedication. The plan they devised fitted the situation in their day and made it possible to witness to the Gospel in an unresponsive society. Indeed, the fact that the situation has changed is testimony to the effectiveness of their planning in its own time.

The Liberian Churches of today, however, cannot rest on their laurels. We live in a new Africa where the old resistance has broken down. The very ones who resisted the Gospel before are now ready to help establish churches in every village. To do this, and to disciple the nation to Christ, the African Church must have a reproducible pattern. To win the masses to Christ, the pattern must be reproducible *among* the masses—that is to say, it must be a pattern that wins the thousands who cannot speak English and who never have had a chance to go to school. Language and literacy are not basic conditions for becoming a Christian, or Christianity would never have started.

A pattern that depends on one missionary for every ten churches it establishes has limited growth potentials. To plant churches in a hundred villages requires ten missionaries, and they just are not available. A pattern that depends on leaders paid by mission funds to establish churches is limited. The source of funds may run dry; funds are always limited. But the indefinitely reproducible pattern suggested here provides each village with a leader the congregation itself can afford to pay, a

man from among the "people" being won. The church building
is one that the congregation can build and repair. Even if the
source of foreign funds dries up, the Church will continue to
expand. Lay leadership is sufficiently trained to lead the village
people to Christ, but not so highly trained that it must live
apart and out of contact with them.

A denomination just beginning work in Liberia, like the
Southern Baptists, has the advantage of being able to start with
a pattern that is indefinitely reproducible. But denominations
with long-established work in Liberia already have a pattern,
and it is impossible to drop everything and start afresh even if it
were desirable. Yet it is possible to modify the pattern so as to
end the stressing of policies that impose limitations on the
multiplication of churches, and to stress, rather, policies that
will develop a pattern that is indefinitely reproducible.

THE DENOMINATIONS

The Church we know is denominations. This is true in
Liberia as in America and most of the rest of the world. "The
denominations" is the form the Church takes in our day. In the
West, where the masses are at least nominally Christian,
ecumenical cooperation that mitigates the offense of denomina-
tionalism is both useful and desirable. But until men are
Christian, ecumenical movements are impossible. Christians
cannot be ecumenical with pagans or Muslims. Until the tribes
are solidly discipled, denominations must continue to work as
denominations. For increase in numbers of men brought to
Christ they have definite advantages. The Church is holy, but to
be holy in the world it must be constantly reformed and
renewed. Denominations accomplish this best. A small denomination is much easier to reform than one great monolithic
Church.

And the denominations reform each other by competition. If
one gets too far out of touch with the needs of men, its members
can always join a more "spiritual" Church around the corner.

If one gets too involved in politics, the others can take
warning from its mistakes and avoid the trap. Or they may,
through Christian fellowship, remind it of its higher allegiances.

This parallel striving keeps the Churches alert. On the other hand, their very variety gives them the flexibility to meet new situations. A denomination can experiment with, let us say, a new method of evangelism; if it is successful, others will copy it. If it is a terrible failure, only one branch has made the blunder and not the whole Church. In evangelism, a denomination might go along for years using faulty methods and assuming that no growth is possible in its particular situation until another denomination comes into the area and, with a slightly different technique, is granted rapid growth. The Holy Spirit is able to show us where He is leading us by the success of the competition. Of course it is possible even for a denomination in such circumstances to refuse to see the truth, to explain the success of the other group as the popularity of false doctrines, and to fall back on the theological excuses for nongrowth mentioned above.

The Church must also be catholic (i.e., inclusive of all types of men). The denominations function to make it all-inclusive. In a society made up of different homogeneous units, tribes, classes, occupations, and so on, one denomination may be so involved in ministering to—let us say—the upper class of the society that it fails to reach the laboring classes. The very fact that it is largely concerned with the upper class may make it difficult for the lower classes to feel at home in it. This can happen to two or even three denominations; but a fourth will arise and see the masses of a different tribe and disciple them. The history of the Church in Liberia includes several examples of this, such as Horton's work among the Bassa in Monrovia, Baker's ministry to the same tribe in Cape Mount, and the move of the Lutherans to serve the Kpelle and Loma in the urban-industrial areas.

Comity or Monopoly? The disadvantage of the denominations for church growth comes not where they are in competition but where they are not. Denominations are the only form of the Church with which we are familiar. This form functions well in an area where each benefits from the competition of others, but it inhibits the spread of the Gospel when one denomination is alone in an area. Unfortunately—because of comity arrangements, isolation, and lack of workers—there are many regions in Liberia where one denomination has total responsibility for preaching the Gospel. In some instances a Church with a monopoly has ignored whole villages for decades, making no attempt whatever to establish churches there until threatened by the spread of a competing Church. Comity agreements were devised in the first place to make sure that the denominations would spread out so as to give as many people as possible the chance of hearing the Gospel. They were never meant to limit the spread of the Church or to reserve certain territory for one denomination in a proprietary sense. When comity agreements are used to stake out territory, they are being misused.

American Protestant missionaries habitually think of their own congregation as having responsibility for only a small part of the community. In their own home town their church was just one of several, sharing the ministry to the spiritual needs of the whole community. In the isolated sections of Liberia they find themselves, and should see themselves, in a *Volkskirche* situation, with the responsibility of being the only Church in the entire area. Their doctrine of the Church does not do justice to the situation. They are used to thinking of it as a small, called-out group. Back home the congregation had perhaps fifty faithful members, and when they get fifty members in Liberia they are inclined to be content and to suppose that they are adequately ministering to the area. What they forget is that at home there were ten other churches in town, each with fifty members or more. In Liberia their congregation is the sole minister of Christ. The result is that the community remains under-churched.

The question is, can one denomination be catholic (i.e., all-inclusive) when it is the only denomination in a village? Where this is so, it must not be content with one church building. Why should there be just one? A single church cannot minister to the needs of the whole community. The one denomination could readily multiply its churches, build several chapels, have several ministers, and serve the community far better. But I do not know of any place in Liberia where this has been done.* Missionaries and pastors usually have a small-denomination mentality. In the monopoly situation, unless Churches resolve to grow and multiply, God, impatient for the tribes' liberation, will probably bring other denominations into their area. This will break comity agreements; but unless the Churches themselves can break out of their small thinking for the sake of souls to be saved, those agreements should be sacrificed.

Adiaphora—or Sacred Cows?

In order to grow, the Churches may have to sacrifice some precious bits of cultural heritage as well. There are forms of worship and all kinds of paraphernalia for doing "mission work." There are budgets permanently apportioned between medical, educational, and evangelistic departments of the mission. There are fine institutions and favorite traditions and a thousand practices. Much of this will have to be changed, even sacrificed, to take advantage of the large opportunities for growth that now exist in Liberia.

All these are what Martin Luther called *adiaphora* (items of religious practice neither forbidden nor enjoined by Scripture and therefore nonessential and left to be determined by custom or individual conscience).[7] The Church can change adiaphora to accommodate itself to the situation. Of course, some things about the Christian faith cannot be changed. But many practices, even ways of thinking about basic doctrines, may be modified without affecting matters of ultimate significance. Unfortunately, "adiaphora" tend to become like the sacred cows of India. To gain the flexibility needed for the Church to grow in the Liberian environment, and to identify with the people, missionaries and pastors will have to learn to distinguish the nonessentials from what is really essential. It is important, for example, that people know Jesus Christ and sing His praise.

* Monrovia, with its many communities, is not homogeneous enough to be considered a single community in the way I use the term here.

[7] Martin Luther, "Of Church Rites," *Book of Concord* (St. Louis, Mo.: Concordia Publishing House, 1957), p. 284.

But it does not matter what tune they use, or whether they are accompanied by a gourd rattle or a pump organ. The nonessentials—even those dear to us—must be sacrificed. This is often one of the costs of church growth.

All too frequently Christians seize one item among the adiaphora—the nonessentials—and raise it up along with more important theological differences as a mark that distinguishes them from some other denomination or from the world. Thus, by association, that item assumes ultimate significance. It becomes a sacred cow. The more this happens, the less flexibility the Church has. Even particular methods of evangelism or the avoidance of them become absolutized, so that individual leaders and whole Churches become bound to a special approach and are not free to try a new one because "it isn't our way of doing things."

St. Paul was free in Christ to be all things to all men, that some might be saved.[8] Methods of evangelism are not of ultimate significance. The Church must be free to experiment, to discover by what method "some may be saved."

Inhibitions to freedom are most obvious in the matter of worship. The so-called liturgical Churches are free to change their liturgical practices, so long as the changes conform to the liturgical movement. Unfortunately, the latter moves only in one direction—that is, toward "high church" practices. They had best not move in the other direction! If they use a musical instrument other than a piano or organ it will call for explanations. And if they speak in tongues, they are in line for censure even if they are moved by the Holy Spirit to do so. On the other hand, the free Churches are just as bound. They may shake rattles and speak in tongues as the Spirit moves, but would be censured if they used a liturgical form for the service—to say nothing of an altar, candles, or a robe—even if the Holy Spirit moved them to do it.

Christianity is like a cup of cold water. Salvation is the water, and the culture in which it is passed is the cup. It is possible that a man will refuse the water because it is in a cup, and he is used to drinking from a gourd dipper; and it is also

[8] I Cor. 9:22.

possible that the missionary, attempting to pass it on in a gourd dipper, will spill the water of life because the utensil is strange to him.

The ways in which Christianity was first given to our forefathers in Europe—that is, the cultural aspects of it—would make us laugh or gasp. But this does not mean that our faith is any less real, or that theirs was. Let us not be afraid to use whatever cup may be at hand to pass on the cold water, nor get excited if at first it is awkwardly held in the hands of the African. And when the African passes on the water to his neighbor in a gourd, let us not forbid that, either.

If the Churches lack flexibility, as we all know, in sharing worship and evangelistic methods across denominational lines within Christendom, there is even greater inflexibility and reserve toward elements from the African culture. But church leaders should acknowledge that "adiaphora are of men"[9] and may be changed for differing circumstances at different times. If this is recognized, then when a tribal man wants to exchange some item of adiaphora for something more indigenous to his culture, the missionary or pastor will not try to forbid it.

Here it is necessary to distinguish between accepting indigenousness and initiating it. A person foreign to the culture should be wary of suggesting such changes. Not knowing the actual usage of an element in the tribal culture, he is likely to make a substitution that is meaningless or even worse. A person unfamiliar with Western culture, for example, might conceivably use an ash tray or a dustpan to take up the offering in church. To those familiar with our culture, his innovation would seem ludicrous if not sacrilegious. Missionaries are likely to make a similar mistake if they go culture-borrowing. On the other hand, Christians who are members of the society will want to make innovations that are proper and acceptable in the eyes of their own people, and usually these will serve to identify the Church with the people.

To have a feast and walk around the town singing after a baptism may seem unimportant, but this was an innovation that helped Loma villagers to identify the joy and significance of

[9] *Ibid.*

baptism in their own cultural terms. Having the feast and taking time out to walk around and sing were small sacrifices for the missionary pastor, since in this case no substitutions were made. When a missionary has to sing the words of a favorite hymn to what for him is an unsingable tune, the novelty is a little more difficult to accept, since he is giving up something. But if he is asked to give up something of which he is proud—or worse yet, to do something he has always been taught not to do—then you are asking him to sacrifice his pride. This is truly difficult, and he will resist making the sacrifice.

Often the growth of the Church depends on just such homely sacrifices. Undoubtedly Peter was proud of the fact that he had never eaten anything the Jews considered "common" or unclean. In Acts 10, when he saw the vision of a sheet full of all kinds of animals and reptiles and birds, and heard a voice saying, "Rise, Peter, kill and eat," he refused. But God spoke austerely to him: "What God has cleansed, do not call common." How strongly Peter must have felt about this matter! If he had not been instructed by direct command to sacrifice his religious practices for the sake of the Gospel, he would never have been willing to go to the house of Cornelius, a pig-eating Gentile. But when he obeyed and yielded up his religious pride, and even did something he had been taught all his life not to do, he had the joy of seeing the Holy Spirit poured out on "even the Gentiles."

Unwilling to sacrifice the adiaphora of our own religious practices (especially our deeply favorite nonessentials), we may in bitter fact miss the wonderful blessing of seeing the Holy Spirit poured out on "a whole people" who are ripe for the Gospel.

CHAPTER VII

ARE MISSIONARIES MORE TROUBLE THAN THEY'RE WORTH?

MOTIVES FOR MISSIONS

Much of the current writing about missions and mission theory boils down to a discussion of the motives for missions—a kind of psychoanalysis of the motivation of missionaries, mission boards, and sending Churches. This self-analysis may clean house for the new patterns of missionary endeavor that will replace some methods of the past that are no longer useful; but it must not be confused with the solution of the problem. A bold new plan is needed in missions. Just such a plan is the rapid expansion of the Church in receptive populations through people movements. The most common charge brought against proponents of this kind of evangelism is that they advocate church growth under the spur of unworthy motives. In the past, certainly, rapid expansion of the Church has sometimes been sparked by wrong motivation. We know, alas, that multitudes can become "Christian" for the wrong reasons. The question is, can multitudes become Christian for the right reasons? In seeking an answer, let us turn briefly to the question of the motive for missions.

Probably the Bible passage most commonly cited as a motive for missions is our Lord's departing command to His disciples: "Go therefore and make disciples of all nations. . . ."[1] Men who have a saving knowledge of Jesus Christ are not content to let others perish. Even if our Lord had not given the great commission to go and make disciples, the Holy Spirit would have impelled His true followers to do so—"that some might be saved." The proper motive for missions is obedience to our Lord's commission, in a Christlike concern for the lost.

This explicit command to go and make disciples is the epitome of apostolic motive for missions. There is hardly a mis-

[1] Matt. 28:19.

157

sionary or a pastor preaching a missionary sermon who has not referred to this text. Young adults and even children in Sunday school are urged to consider what the command to go means for them. Missionaries make recruiting speeches about going. Pastors preach mission messages about going. And finally, when some young person actually does stand up and say, "All right, I'll go," everyone is overcome with joy at the wonder of it. His friends make such a fuss about his being willing to go, and he himself is so impressed with his new status as one who has decided to go, and is so busy getting ready, that when he finally does arrive at his destination it may be several years before he seriously thinks to ask, "What was the going *for*?

The going is to "make disciples." Going into all the world is only half the commission. The other half is to "make disciples." The great commission is not carried out simply by a change of place, if no disciples are made. Winning disciples is never as easy as the mere going; it is difficult, sometimes almost impossible. And so after several years of trying unsuccessfully by various methods to make disciples, the missionary may allow his goals to shift subtly and seek other results to justify his having come. As a missionary, I am familiar with the subtle pressures on us—and sometimes not so subtle—to modify our goals. I am sure that Liberian pastors and village Christians are subject to similar pressures, which in their own way tend to modify their goals. The overall result of this process may be a distortion of the goal, and even of the Church's motive for mission.

I am indebted to Dr. James Scherer for his lucid exposition of three distortions of the missionary motive: political, cultural, and ecclesiastical, in his book *Missionary Go Home*—the chapter entitled "The Right Thing for the Wrong Reasons."[2]

POLITICAL DISTORTIONS

Throughout the last two thousand years or so there have been times when missionaries were sent and men became Christians for political reasons. "Mission then becomes the process by

[2] James A. Scherer, *Missionary Go Home* (Englewood Cliffs, N.J.: Prentice-Hall, 1964), Chap. II, pp. 27-39.

which Christendom is extended. The political and spiritual realms advance together."[3] Constantine, Charlemagne, and the conquistadors are blatant examples of the political motive for missions recorded in history.

This is quite obvious to our modern sensitivities. Present-day Liberian churchmen and missionaries are too sophisticated to make the conspicuous mistakes of the past. But it is possible to have false motives even in present-day Liberia. Though the temptation may be camouflaged, it is just as real. If Christian leaders recognize the pressures that exist and where they come from, they will be better able to resist them.

Most of Liberia's political leaders are church members. The tribal people are not likely to distinguish between Church and state or between Christ and culture. The Loma people, for example, call everything foreign to their culture *wui faa*— literally, "imported matters." *Wui faa* includes government, Western culture, and Christianity—in the Loma mind: foreign rule, foreign ways, and foreign religion. There has been deep-seated suspicion of and resistance to all *wui faa*. But the tribal people are no longer resisting the government, and there is a corresponding breakdown of the resistance to Western culture and Christianity. In fact, it is very likely that the same identification that caused them to reject Christianity as the religion of foreigners, when they were resisting all *wui faa*, will cause them to accept it now that *wui faa* is being accepted.

It is very probable that some will now become Christians hoping to have better relationships with their political leaders by doing so. I have heard lay evangelists, urging the pagan tribesmen to become Christians, mention as one good reason the fact that President Tubman is a Christian, and therefore anyone who wants to be a loyal citizen ought also to become a Christian. Evangelists can be taught that this is not the reason to become a Christian. But once the idea has moved into the popular mind, it is difficult to dissociate this motive from the mission of the Church or at least from the people's understanding of it.

This confusion is by no means limited to the tribal people. Several of the pastors I interviewed mentioned it as one of the

[3] *Ibid.*, p. 27.

problems of the Church. The President and Vice President are in fact active churchmen. Other political leaders, however, sometimes think that because they are influential and hold important positions in the government, they should have corresponding authority and influence in the Church. Or vice versa—men who have important church connections sometimes feel that this entitles them to political privileges and favors. When the Church allows political motives to infringe upon or replace its apostolic motive for missions, it is acting unworthily and often fails to fulfill its prophetic role. A pastor will not speak out against injustices if his salary is paid by, or he expects favors from, the one perpetrating the injustices.

The fragmentation of tribalism is one of Liberia's disabling difficulties. Christianity is potentially a strong unifying force in the country. And Christians are good and obedient citizens. As St. Peter said, "Be submissive to every human institution . . . the emperor as supreme."[4] If Christians were willing to submit to a pagan emperor in Peter's time, how much more willing will they be to submit to the Christian leader of a modern nation? The idea that the tribes should be evangelized in order to unify the nation is a constant pressure to distort the apostolic motive for missions. When all the tribes do become Christian and there is a church in every village, the country undoubtedly will be more unified. But this unity must always be a resultant benefit of the mission and never the main reason or motive for planting the Church.

In Liberia the government still looks to the Churches and missions to provide education and medical care for a large number of its citizens. It contributes funds to the support of such church-affiliated institutions as hospitals and schools, and there is constant and explicit pressure on the Churches to fill a primarily culturizing and civilizing role. It is good for Churches and missions to engage in charitable works (schools, clinics, and literacy campaigns), but the fact is that they are required to do so by the Liberian Constitution; this is the price of their acceptance in the country, which makes it very hard to judge whether

[4] I Pet. 2:13.

such works are performed primarily out of Christian love or simply to conform to political pressure.

CULTURAL DISTORTIONS

Cultural distortion of the motive for missions takes place when Christianity is confused with culture—in this case, the culture of the West. "Mission now becomes a permeation of the benighted lands of Asia and Africa with Christian culture and moral standards. The missionary is the bearer of the values of another society."[5]

Jesus said, ". . .man shall not live by bread alone."[6] He refused to found His Kingdom by turning stones into bread. That did not stop him from feeding the five thousand when they were in need. But he did not make filling their stomachs His main work, and He left when they came to take Him by force and make Him a king. It is easy enough for missionaries to decry making rice Christians, but in the modern confusion between Christianity and culture a good deal more is involved than mere rice. It is not always easy to recognize the cultural motive for mission as it replaces the apostolic.

The benefits of Western culture, notably education and medicine, are so obviously superior to the bush school and the witch doctor that the Church is constantly tempted to use them to found the Kingdom, or even let them become a substitute for the Kingdom. Every Church and mission carries on evangelistic programs as well as their other activities. But it is precisely these evangelistic programs that have not been successful. Sometimes we use success in the field of medicine and education as a cover-up for our notably unsuccessful attempts at evangelism. Evangelism can and must be more effective. Indeed, unless it is so, the other works of the Church will be, in very truth, to no avail.

Offering welfare services and other charitable works is one way of being useful and getting a hearing in the pagan community. The people are poor, illiterate, and often sick, and most missionaries feel somewhat guilty about the creature comforts

[5] Scherer, *op. cit.*, p. 31.
[6] Luke 4:4.

they themselves enjoy by comparison with the circumstances of the people around them.* Add to this the fact that the government itself requires missions to do eleemosynary works, and it is not difficult to understand the pressures on the Church to become a civilizing institution rather than the messenger of the Gospel.

When Lutheran missionaries first came to Zorzor in 1923, they gave gifts of soap to anyone who would come to the hospital. In some places, fathers were encouraged by gifts of money to send their children to school. No one has to be bribed any longer. Almost a thousand village women went to Zorzor hospital to have their babies in 1964. I was present at a district council in that town when every chief whose town had as yet no school rose and pleaded with the Secretary of the Interior to establish a public school in his own area. Missionaries must ask themselves if they really desire the nations and tongues of Liberia to "confess that Christ is Lord to the glory of God the Father."[7] Are they really concerned that the poor have the Gospel preached to them? Do they truly desire that the grace of God reach out to those masses—that they be bound on earth so as to be bound in heaven? Or is education, after all, what the missionaries really believe in?

Indeed, the missions have converted whole populations already—not to the Gospel, but to values of Western medicine and education. The acceptance of secular culture continues apace; but alas, it is only bread, and "man shall not live by bread alone." Christ refused to give in to the temptation to establish His Kingdom through bread or miracles. The Church today is tempted as He was tempted, and too often yields to the urgent impulse to give the bread that perishes instead of the imperishable Word. Western missionaries with technological accomplishments awe the villagers as if to put God to the test, and as if they no longer believed Jesus' admonition: ". . .seek ye first

---

* This is part of the "culture shock" discussed in the following pages. In the interviews, several missionaries expressed the need of making sacrifices in order to identify with the culture of the people.
[7] Phil. 2:11.

the Kingdom of God, and his righteousness; and all these things shall be added unto you."[8]

When missionaries first came and saw whole villages full of children whose latent talents must remain latent, since there were no schools, they would have been less than Christian if they had not set up schools. When they saw the suffering—the sick and the mourners sorrowing for those who had died from preventable causes—they would not have been worthy of the name of Christ if they had not provided hospitals and clinics for healing mortal illness. In Liberia today, however, the government is rapidly moving to provide these services for all its citizens. But it will never establish churches for the proclamation of the Gospel in the villages. Unless the denominations and missions recognize that their primary responsibility is for the Word of God, the masses in Liberia will perforce try to live on very ordinary bread.

If missionaries spend their time and efforts in the service of educational and medical institutions without making disciples of the nations, they freeze forever the relationship between the givers and the receivers.[9] As long as "selfless" missionaries give their lives in self-sacrificing service, the villagers will remain content to take what is given, be thankful, and go back to the village until they need the services of the good missionaries again. If, on the other hand, the people are given the Gospel and their whole family or village becomes Christian, they themselves will have the spiritual resources for selflessness which will make possible their own development and their own works of mercy. When a son grows up in a Christian family, he has a strength and depth of character far superior to that of the boy who belongs half to the pagan world and half to the world of the missionaries. When we missionaries set up large institutions for medical work and education among winnable peoples who *are not being won*, we may gain the plaudits of the people, but we are not really giving them the best we have: the Gospel, which is the very source of those good things.

[8] Matt. 6:33.
[9] Allen, *Spontaneous Expansion of the Church*, p. 46.

To want to continue in the role of the rich uncle is to want the poor nephew to remain forever in the subservient role of grateful receiver of all the good things that flow from our hand. This is playing God, a danger for every doctor, nurse, and educator—and, I must include, every pastor—a danger for everyone who represents the givers in a needy world.

What happens when the time comes when foreign missionaries must leave a country, as they were forced to leave China? A few trained leaders will continue the work and pass it on to other generations. But will the whole people, made new by the resources and strength of the Gospel, be able to wait out the winter of world events until spring? This question is especially pertinent if, as has happened in China and parts of the Congo, the trained and intellectual Christian leaders are rounded up and shot. The imminent possibility of political upheaval destroying institutions which have been built in advance of the Church (and in too many cases independently of whatever small Church exists) is a danger well recognized by most missionaries. But the challenge facing them today is whether or not they are willing to modify their present program, the better to prepare for such a possibility. Too often in the daily pressure of meeting unlimited demands with limited resources, the major missionary purpose of the Church, which is to disciple the nations to Christ, is replaced by a cultural motive.

I am not here suggesting that the Church abandon its institutions and merciful works. On the contrary, it is my personal feeling that many of them should be improved and expanded. It will probably be necessary for the Church to support these institutions during the foreseeable future, as one of the best ways to give meaning to the love of Christ which it confesses. However, institutions have a way of becoming self-propelled and going off, each in its own direction. The institutions are to be the servants of the Church and not the masters. When the true perspective becomes clouded, the institutions themselves exert a powerful force to subvert the motives of the Church's mission. They play such an important role in Liberia, where missions for a hundred years have carried the major burden of education, where the government still requires them to found hospitals and schools, and where the needs of the tribal people are so great, that the Churches must be doubly on guard against cultural distortion of the motive of missions, which this emphasis on institutions is likely to bring about.

As long as the tribal masses remain largely unconverted, the institutions will rightly or wrongly be considered as tools in the process of conversion. But as soon as the masses of the people become Christians, they will understand the institutions of the Church as part of God's grace to them. Social enterprises that serve a "Christian" population are supported by it—if not through church offerings, then through taxes collected by the government. Under these conditions they assume an entirely different role.

When the tribal people become Christians, there will be an even greater need for schools and hospitals. No one wants a Christian population which long remains unable to read the Bible. The hundreds of village Christians cannot develop vital congregations unless they are nurtured by an extensive school system. But developing an extensive school system before the Church is planted is putting the cart before the horse.

Institutions Properly Follow the Church. The institutions of the Church fulfill their proper function when they nurture the Church. When they precede it, they are likely to distort the motive for missions and undermine the Church's faith. The danger of self-deception is great. At times the Church seems to be growing—or it is hoped that it will grow—because of education (and in places it does grow a little in this way). Then the large school system is defended on the grounds that it is evangelistically effective. But exactly at this point arises the greatest danger of identifying conversion to Christianity with getting an education and adopting Western ways, and here the cultural distortion of the motive for missions becomes most pressing.

Institutional programs are no more important than other programs that promote the Church's mission; but they tend to assume a significance out of proportion to their actual contribution to the life of the Church. This is true, first of all, because they represent a relatively large financial investment, which gives them permanence. It is possible to start evangelistic work in a new village with almost no financial investment at all. And it requires very little trouble to move the work to a more responsive area when opportunity presents itself. But it takes large capital investment to set up a hospital or a school, and administrators will expend more energy to keep from closing an institution than was put forth to open it in the first place. This permanence also makes the enterprise inflexible in responding to changing needs.

Second, institutions demand and get top priority on men and money. The most capable young national leaders are diverted from the ministry into their service. These heads of institutions have influence in the affairs of the Church that is often greater than their churchmanship warrants. Because of their close alliance and dependence, there is a real danger that missionaries and nationals alike will mistake the institutions for the Church. Teachers and nurses in missionary establishments sometimes feel that, since they are serving the institutions of the Church, it is unnecessary for them to attend the worship services of the congregation or participate in its evangelistic outreach.

Quite unintentionally, of course, institutions in advance of the Church tend to distort the motive of missions in the minds of potential converts. Instead of helping to communicate the Gospel, institutions sometimes conceal it. Where there is a fifty-thousand-dollar hospital with a staff of fifty and a thirty-thousand-dollar school with a staff of ten in the same town as a two-thousand-dollar church with a staff of one (almost full-time pastor), it is easy for village people to get a "wrong" idea of what the missionary thinks is really important.

And when the cultural motive for missions predominates, their idea may not be so far wrong. A good test of what missionaries think is important is their conversation. When they get together, what do they talk about? Making disciples of the nation, and the spiritual problems of new Christians? Or do they talk almost entirely about the institutions they are running? People talk about what they care about—what they think is really important. Too many missions have only a few people who talk about making disciples, and too many who talk about developing institutions.

Mission enterprises usually start out with the best of motives. It may be said that almost all missionaries begin their work sincerely intending to win men to Christ. But under the pressure of trying to meet unlimited human needs with limited resources and their own growing uncertainty as to the goals of missions, their energy often gets tied up in all kinds of good mission activity. Institutions are built which must be continued. Even if a missionary wants to plant churches, he is saddled with maintaining a school system that was started by his predecessors. The generation that founded the mission to preach the Gospel dies out, and a new generation grows up, trained to work at some specialty and to raise money to keep the mission going. This subtle change of goals is deadly to the growth of the Church. A drastic re-examination of the goal, and whether what they are doing is likely to achieve it, is a must for all missions, Churches, board secretaries, and missionaries.

ECCLESIASTICAL DISTORTIONS

The Church, which is the Body of Christ, also has an institutional form. Promoting it may in itself become an unworthy motive for missions. The apostolic motive of the mission of the Church must not be distorted into an ecclesiastical motive. This happens when missionaries build the Kingdom to the glory of the institutional Church—or, more particularly, their own denomination. Proclaiming the Gospel of salvation is replaced here by the reproduction of the pattern of the Mother Church, down to the last detail of theology, polity, ministerial training, and even ways of raising money. This is ecclesiastical ethnocentrism, the most subtle of unworthy motives for missions. Missionaries are especially vulnerable to it. They are likely to renounce political pressures for conversion, whether direct or indirect, because they seem crass. They are aware of the dangers of making rice Christians and so avoid some of the cultural pressures. But planting the Church just as it was back home—this is likely to win their full support. We have already seen examples of it in the preceding chapter.

In Liberia political unity is desirable. Education, medical care, and welfare services are desirable. Having a congregation in every village, with a fine building and a trained pastor paid by his flock, is also desirable. If the Church faithfully carries out her apostolic mission, all these benefits and more will be hers as well. But they must always be the result of missions—not the reason for them.

MIXED MOTIVES AND GOD'S GRACE

I have discussed the pitfalls of unworthy motives for missions into which Christians are likely to fall. When one examines oneself in the Liberian situation, one is forced to recognize that one's own motives and those of converts are always mixed. But with all these false motives described and confessed, how can we speak of the rapid expansion of the Church in people-movement fashion without being cynical?

To suggest something so apparently bold and brash as the rapid expansion of the Church by people movements can only be saved from cynicism if we take God's grace seriously. In the final analysis, the Kingdom of God does not depend on our motives, but on His grace. It is a common experience to begin a task, or make a decision, which at the time seems exactly the right thing to do—a veritable stroke of genius—then a week or a month or even a year later, to look back and realize that what one did was a mistake—if not quite the worst thing one could have done under the circumstances. Planning for the growth of the Church is a formidable task, involving dozens of decisions. We dare not rush in carelessly; but after we have studied and prepared, we must dare to decide and act on our decision, trusting in God's grace. If what we did turns out to be sin, then (as Martin Luther wrote to Melanchthon), "Be a sinner and sin boldly, but believe and rejoice in Christ even more boldly, for He is victorious over sin, death and the world."[10] We must recognize that even when we do the best we know how to do, we are certainly still less than perfect. We always fall short of the glory of God. We make mistakes; only God can correct them. God

[10] Martin Luther, "To Philipp Melanchthon, Wartburg, August 1, 1521," *Luther's Works*, Vol. 48, *Letters I* (Philadelphia: Fortress Press, 1963), p. 282.

will have to forgive us and correct our mistakes for His will to be accomplished.

This does not excuse us from examining our motives most carefully. A Christian must never deliberately choose to convert men for unworthy reasons. Nor can anything be substituted for the message of the cross. On the other hand, "nothing will be able to separate us from the love of God in Christ Jesus"[11]—not even our own mixed motives. We will never be perfect, and if we wait to proclaim the Gospel until our motives are perfect, we will be paralyzed into inaction. This is the danger of the self-analysis school of mission theorists. If we succumb to it, we will find ourselves guilty not only of impure motives but of disobedience as well.

Our Lord's direct command is to go and make disciples. The proclamation of the Gospel must not come to a halt just because the preacher has human motives. Nor must the hearers be refused because they have human motives. The Gospel is always carried in earthen vessels. God saves men, not because their motives and programs are pure, but because ardently and urgently He loves the lost. He can use us as channels of His grace to reach out to the lost, even though He has to do it while we ourselves are much less than perfect. In fact, those who are too careful that their motives and methods should be perfect are in danger of trusting in themselves rather than in God.

The grace of God is bigger than men's motives, and able to overcome them. In Liberia, God may use the impulses of a politician seeking political advantage to open doors for those who bear the message of the Gospel. When a chief allows Christian missionaries to preach only because they have the approval of the central government in Monrovia, those who receive the Gospel are saved nevertheless. When a chief becomes a Christian for political advantage, it does not prevent God from changing him and his subjects through the power of the Gospel. The same thing happens in the fields of education and medicine. Because a boy originally went to the mission school merely for the advantages of an education does not mean that God cannot transform him into an outstanding leader of the

[11] Rom. 8:39.

Church. When a person comes to the mission hospital to be
healed of an ailment, God is able to use the witness of those
working at the hospital to heal his spirit as well.

The motives of persons who come into the Church in the
large numbers accompanying a people movement are often
mixed, but no more so than the motives of those who come one
at a time. When in a village a large number want to become
Christians, it will be discovered that they are impelled by all
kinds of reasons. Some hope that this new God will help them
in their relation to the government. Others hope that the mission
will send them a teacher for a school or a nurse for a clinic.
Others may have a magical notion of the benefits of having a
church in their village. On top of these unworthy motives *they
also believe that Christ died to save them from everlasting
death.*[12] If a missionary decides that he will not baptize these
people simply because some of their motives are impure, he
allows the impure motives to assume ultimate significance and
keep them out of the Kingdom. When we discover that what we
thought was a wonderful outpouring of the Spirit in a village is
tainted by unworthy motives, and are shocked nearly into inaction because we are afraid the whole tribe may be the same—
then let us "sin boldly" and trust God, who loves the lost,
motive-tainted converts, to work His miracle of grace—as He
has in our own lives.

THE MISSIONARY

The twenty-two missions and mission societies in Liberia
have more than two hundred missionaries.* The tasks at which
they labor are so varied and the circumstances so different that
it is impossible to catalog all or even most of the ways in which
missionaries, by their foreignness, affect the growth of the
Church. The missionaries and pastors I have interviewed were
primarily those serving parishes in the tribal villages. From
those interviews and the expressed concerns of the pastors involved, I have singled out for discussion here some of the

[12] Pickett, *Christian Mass Movements*, pp. 155-68.
* This figure includes some missionary wives.

important problems affecting church growth that are seldom mentioned.

One of the common explanations for the slow growth of the Church is the shortage of personnel. Liberia gets its full quota of missionaries, but many of them do not stay long. Every major denomination in the country has experienced a relatively high rate of turnover in missionary personnel compared to other fields. Housing, climate, health—all have been cited as reasons for it, but the inability to communicate because of lack of language study, the pressure of running institutions, and the disappointing results of the mission-station approach are equally important factors. Whatever the reasons, the resulting discontinuity in program is one element contributing to the slow growth of the churches.[13]

Having recognized this, we must not imagine that an increase of missionary personnel is the solution to the problem. The Church grows best when the pattern of growth is indefinitely reproducible. Missionary personnel are necessarily a limited resource, and therefore not indefinitely reproducible. A pattern of church expansion that depends on increasing the number of missionaries as the main source of growth will never result in the kind of growth necessary to disciple the tribes in Liberia.

Even if sufficient numbers were available, it is erroneous to expect that mere multiplication of missionaries would result in church growth. If the additional members of the missionary staff have been trained to accept, and be satisfied with, the little growth that accompanies the mission-station approach, increases in staff will only result in increases in mission work, and not in greater growth of the Church.

In Liberia, where rapid growth of the Church has usually seemed an impossibility, missionaries have developed slogans to justify the small church growth and so fortify them in their dogged determination to stick to the post. A common one is, "One soul is worth all this effort." As rapid expansion of the Church becomes possible, we missionaries need new slogans. Why not say, "If we can win a thousand, why be satisfied with fifty"—to help us break the chains of small expectations?

[13] From an interview with Harvey J. Currens, June 1964.

Some missionaries contribute to the slow growth of the Church by their failure to communicate. The prime example of this has already been mentioned: namely, those who never find time to learn the language of the people. This point has been so often stressed and so well argued that it seems strange that the majority of missionaries working in the tribal areas of Liberia are still hobbled in their work by inadequate command of the languages. Many know no tribal language at all.

In some areas the Church could grow rapidly if the missionaries spent more time in the villages, where growth is taking place, rather than being tied down to administration of a mission station. In districts where the missionary has supervisory responsibilities for several villages, success will require that he actually get into them. Some of the most effective church planting in Liberia is taking place where a supervising missionary or Liberian pastor spends two weeks or more on path trips in isolated villages. For the villagers to know that the missionary understands and lives with them, and that a strong man has his finger on the pulse of the situation, is important. There is no substitute for men of supervisory status—Liberian pastors or foreign missionaries—spending time in the field.

National pastors often learn from missionaries. When they observe that a pastor's role is to sit at a desk and that evangelism is a task for lowly paid workers only, a severe blow is dealt to the Church. Some parishes in Liberia have grown almost not at all because of this attitude.[14] And specialists in the field of literacy, youth work, Sunday school, or teachers at Bible schools and seminaries, will find no real substitute for actual visits to the village where their theories and programs meet their severest test: application in the lives of the congregations.

Sometimes missionaries stand in the way of rapid expansion of the Church because they are overly protective. They are afraid of growth for fear it will not be solid enough, and imagine that a congregation must continue in the same doctrinal position and constellation of membership from the day of its founding until the last trumpet blows. Thus emphasis on the need for slow, solid growth makes missionaries extremely cau-

[14] Bowers interview (cf. p. 141, n. 36).

tious. They dare not let the Church expand where they cannot be there to supervise every major move, and too often the minor ones as well.[15]

In the history of an average congregation in Europe or America there are members who come out of other congregations— even other denominations. There are sometimes splits and disagreements, as well as reconciliations and restorations. All are part of the natural life of congregations. There is no reason to expect them to be different in Liberia. To the extent that the missionary keeps everything moving along smoothly so that there are no dissensions, splits, or trials to challenge the faith of the members, he is pampering the local church like a hothouse plant. If he is ever forced to leave his post as supervisor, this frail plant will have less chance of survival than a neighbor which has been in contact with the real world all the time.

Missionaries contribute to the slow growth of the Church also when they are concerned only with relatively short-term goals: the day-by-day routine of getting Communion to a village, visiting the sick, writing a report, attending a committee meeting. Ideally their goal is for every person in every village in their area to become a Christian, or at least to have the real option of becoming one. For most missionaries that goal seems so remote that it never seriously enters their planning for either the immediate or the distant future. Without planning for the conversion of whole villages they cannot move rapidly toward that goal; it is so far from their minds that they do not even seriously consider it in their prayers, and never ask themselves what might happen or what it might be like if a whole village, a whole clan, a whole extended family became Christian. In fact if, by God's grace, movement toward this goal occurs and the Church begins to grow rapidly, they are likely to be taken by surprise and to wonder if what is happening is sound.

Cultural Overhang. Missionaries are foreigners. Their own middle-class American culture patterns sometimes prevent them from seeing the church growth potential among tribal Liberians. The missionary when he first arrives on the field is likely to be

[15] Allen, *op. cit.,* p. 57.

thrown into a state of cultural shock by what he sees.[16] After a period of orientation he adjusts his thinking to take account of these new facts of life. Too often he takes the culture of the people seriously only to the extent of marking it down in his mind as a mistake to be corrected and changed.

In this process of reaction, the criterion for rejecting a particular aspect of a people's culture is less likely to be the Gospel than the culture of the missionary's home country. But the fact is, if it were possible to go back in time, the missionary would probably be just as shocked by the culture and practices of New Testament church communities as by those of a tribal village in Liberia. Readiness for Christianity was never intended to be measured by nonessential culture patterns—and cannot be. There is a great danger that the missionary will find himself attacking particular aspects of a culture not because they are unbiblical or un-Christian, but simply because they are so totally different from what he knows in his own culture. This attitude on his part causes people to be unnecessarily offended at the Gospel. The more powerful an institution in the tribal society, the more likely the missionary is to cause offense by his reactions.

The extended family is perhaps the strongest institution in the life of the tribal man. The missionaries teach the commandment, "Honor thy father and mother . . . ," which is supposed to buttress the family. But if the missionary, not recognizing extended family-oriented values in the tribal culture, demands practices that support only the individualistic values of his own American society, he is undermining this very institution of the family in the tribal background.

I remember hearing of a missionary whose cook belonged to a large, rather influential family. The missionary complained that his man could never "get ahead" or save any money because members of his family were always coming and making demands on him which he obediently met. When the missionary was transferred to another station, he urged the cook to come

[16] See Luzbetak, *The Church and the Cultures,* p. 97 for an excellent discussion in which he differentiates also between "going native," "anti-native," and "empathy and identification."

along to where he would be free from demanding family ties. In effect, he was encouraging the man to look out for his own interests—to "get ahead"—at the expense of the family he had been taught to honor from childhood. This may be the same missionary who, when his cook left him on short notice for a better-paying job, complained that "Africans have no sense of responsibility."

Almost every missionary has a story like this to tell about the inconsistencies of someone else's cultural overhang (the term is a sober and correct one for this phenomenon). In a moment of honesty we must all admit that we, too, are guilty of similar cultural perpetuations, carried over from the setting that is native to us. It must also be noted here that the tribal people, at least in the Loma tribe with which I am familiar, will with great patience bend over backward to apologize for the unthinking mistakes of the foreigner in their midst. But constant mistakes do not commend the Gospel to the pagan world.

POLYGAMY AND THE MISSIONARY

Missionaries who even unconsciously insist on their own cultural pattern and values place unnecessary stumbling blocks in the way of converts and raise unnecessary barriers to the rapid expansion of the Church. When this happens, the aspects of tribal culture that differ most conspicuously from the culture pattern of the West get blown up out of all proportion to their actual significance in tribal society and become major obstacles to the growth of the Church. Polygamy has become just such an obstacle to church growth in Liberia, and indeed in most of Africa south of the Sahara. Every missionary pastor I interviewed who is working among the tribal people mentioned polygamy as one of the major problems facing the Church, and hardly any of them were sure that they had the final solution.

Let it be said at once that there is, of course, no question here of justifying polygamy as a way of life. The question is rather of how to deal with situations that were honorably set up within a culture by its own norms, before the Christian alternative was known or confronted—a culture which literally *has no place*, economic or personal, for a woman turned out of a polygamous household in order to reduce it to monogamy. Not to mention the effect on the children. It must be remembered that the finest, most upright personalities within a culture may be involved in the custom, so that their households in other respects show qualities—warmth and mutual love and concern— which would normally be a good basis for Christian life; qualities which also hinder them from making cruel disposition of each other.

This grossly incomplete statement of a complex and in some sense innocent problem, which is painful and thorny in almost every direction, should suffice to show, however, that in considering how to deal with it we will need to draw on every resource of Christian understanding. How the transition to a Christian monogamous way of life is to be accomplished requires the most careful and sensitive thought and the guidance of the Holy Spirit.

The Old Testament accepted polygamy but forbade adultery. King David knew the Mosaic law against adultery, yet had many wives.[17] God judged him, not for his many wives but for taking Bathsheba, the wife of another man. The New Testament does not even mention polygamy except in the case of I Timothy 3:2 and 12 where "let the bishops be the husbands of one wife" has historically been understood to mean that the Church teaches that church leaders could not be polygamists, perhaps contrasting them with ordinary laymen. Such a rule would still have been necessary at the time I Timothy was written, since polygamy was still to be found among the Jews and was quite common in pagan communities.[18] If polygamy is as important as contemporary missionaries in Africa have made it out to be, it is amazing that New Testament writers, who faced the same situation, said so little about it. For readers who think it an academic question, for which the simple, automatic answer is cut and dried, I offer the following case study from my parish.

[17] II Sam. 15:16.
[18] Walter Lock, *The Pastoral Epistles,* "International Critical Commentary" series (New York: Charles Scribner's Sons, 1924), p. 36, referring to Justin Martyr, *Tryph C,* 134.

Mulbah is about fifty years of age. He has two wives. The first, Gbolu, is in her mid-forties. His mother's brother helped him "buy" her when he was a young man. "Buy" is a Loma euphemism meaning to marry. It does not carry the same distasteful connotation in Loma as in English; indeed, this uncle gave Mulbah his own daughter and made the bride price very reasonable. This is the custom.

Gbolu is a good and faithful wife. She works hard and, except for the time when she was sick—the time they carried her to the hospital—she has never failed to cook rice for his supper or prepare his bath. Their first two children died. After that she bore him a son who was strong and "stayed." The young man is clever and works hard to obey and help his father with the farm. He is old enough to be seeking a wife for himself now.

Gbolu's second living child is a daughter. She has now grown up to be a strikingly attractive girl and has many suitors. She will certainly choose one soon. Her other son is in high school. Mulbah and his family have sacrificed every year to pay the tuition for this boy to go to the mission school, to buy books and clothes, and to pay for the room and board. Blood, sweat, and tears have gone into keeping him in school, but it will be worth it, for he has done well. In a tribal society, where less than one per cent of the population goes to high school, this is no small achievement.

When this last son was born, Gbolu got her aunt's oldest daughter to come and live with Mulbah and be his "friend." Yassah was a good, obedient girl and very helpful when the baby was born. At Gbolu's urging, Mulbah spoke to Yassah's father and marriage arrangements were made. It is not uncommon for the pressure to take another wife to originate with the first wife, for a variety of reasons: in order to have help with the farm work, or to content her husband during the long periods of enforced sexual abstinence following pregnancy (by tribal custom, three years with a girl until she is weaned, four years for a boy), and so on. Yassah's own children are a girl of ten who helps the women with the cooking and washing, a boy of seven who will begin public school next year, and a baby boy who has just learned to walk. God has indeed been good to Mulbah. He has a fine family—four sons and two daughters—and he loves them all very much.

Two years ago an evangelist-preacher came to Mulbah's town and was given a house in the same quarter. Mulbah instinctively liked the young man and his wife, and since the God palaver (preaching and singing) was just across the way, he could hear the sermons and witnessing without even leaving his porch. Last year something the evangelist said—or perhaps it was the kindness of the missionary doctor at the hospital where his wife Gbolu was helped so much—or perhaps even because his own brother became a Christian in a neighboring town, and his son is in mission school—for some reason Mulbah started attending services. One Sunday night last month a visiting preacher came to their town for special services of preaching. Mulbah's young wife, Yassah, was one of those who "stood before God" to join the baptismal class and learn about God palaver. When she learns the lessons, they will pour God's water on her head, and she will go to heaven when she dies. Even the missionary, who has a hard time speaking Loma, said the same thing himself.

Mulbah wants to have God's water poured on his head too. He is sure that Jesus is the one who can protect him from evil and from Satan. But Mulbah is very troubled because he knows that to become a Christian he will have to choose between Gbolu and Yassah. How can a man choose between his first wife—the mother of his son who is in high school, his beautiful daughter, and his older son who helps him with the farm work—and the mother of his other children, including the little toddling baby who is just learning to say "Mulbah"?*

In the face of the rule that forbids baptism to polygamists, three alternatives are open to him: (a) Get rid of one wife. (b) Pretend to get rid of one wife. (c) Remain outside the community of baptized believers. Is it really God's will for a man, who has made a solemn promise to the fathers of his two wives, to be cut off from the fellowship of the saints and the love of God because he is unwilling to break that promise? And that the man whose promise means little or who happens to have a sick

* Loma children call their parents by their given names.

and barren wife should put her away and receive the commendation of the missionaries?

And what about the woman who is put away? Our Lord said, "If any man divorces his wife, he causes her to commit adultery." In the Loma culture this is certainly the case, for there is no place in it for single women. Every divorced woman must, of necessity, go into the household of some other man. In effect, the husband forces her into adultery. In a large majority of cases, when forced into such a decision, the men give up the older wife (though a few missions have a rule that a man must keep his first wife and put away all others). I suppose for the children's sake this might often be best, since the younger ones need their father more than those who are grown. Yet it is tragic for the children also to break up the home.

Where the Church or mission has this kind of rule, the missionary who is least fluent in the language is likely to be least aware of the problem. In fact, he may have a long list of men who have given up their wives and are now "living as Christians should." Some make a show of giving up their other wives and build a second house for them in another corner of the town. The non-Christian villagers wink about them and laugh at the missionary behind whose back these deceptions go on. But they do not think highly of a religion that results in such actions. Then there are some who will not lie to the missionaries nor break their promise to their wives and families, and who are therefore burdened to their grave with the strange choice between a cultural practice that has been accepted for generations and the arbitrary rules of missionary Christianity.

For the missionaries the greatest danger is that they will become hair-splitting legalists like the Pharisees, willing to cross seas and mountains to make a single convert, and then lay on them burdens that they themselves are not called upon to bear.[19] For the Church the danger is that the hypocrisy of those who pretend to live in one way and are in reality living in another will destroy her integrity and dilute her witness. For the convert there is the danger that this will burden

[19] Matt. 23:15, paraphrased to soften Jesus' own language.

his conscience with a yoke that is not easy and a burden that is far from light.

For the pagan community the danger is that the emphasis on polygamy will conceal the real "offense" of the Gospel. For the pagan the distinction is apt to be, not between those who follow Christ and those who do not, but between those who practice polygamy and those who do not. The missionaries have tried to reject polygamy by rejecting polygamists.

By the very stringency of their method they have unwittingly guaranteed that polygamy will remain in the society as a respected alternative to Christianity. This accepted social norm will unite a segment of the community and insulate its members from the Gospel. They will not even think of themselves as potential converts—the Gospel's decision will not be a possibility for them. This group of rejected polygamists will form a social backwater, a reservoir in which the old religious sacrifices and fears will continue to breed, a pocket of resistance to the Gospel. These pockets are particularly susceptible to conversion to Islam. By encouraging a man to give up his wife, the Church is in the position of encouraging a man to turn his back on responsibilities. Surely the Gospel should not force him to choose between honor—that is, his responsibility to a wife and children—and his own salvation.

The grace of God will not be bound in the cultural box of Western social patterns. If uncircumcised, pig-eating Gentiles can receive the Holy Spirit and be baptized,[20] then by the grace of God polygamists can become Christians without being forced to thrust a wife into adultery or break a serious and honorable promise to a wife's father and family. They can become Christians with the full assurance of salvation that comes from believing and being baptized, and communing with the faithful. To deny this is to doubt the power of God's grace.

There is plenty in the Gospel of Christ to cause offense without burdening it with unnecessary legalism. If a man is lost, let it be because he refused to accept Christ as his risen Lord

[20] Acts 10:44.

and Savior, and not because he loved both his wives too much to disgrace and ruin them, or was too upright to lie, or live in deceit.

Up until 1951 the Lutheran Church in Liberia refused to baptize the men in polygamous households. In that year, in an effort to eliminate unnecessary offense to the Gospel and to relieve unnecessarily burdened consciences, the Lutheran Church in Liberia adopted a statement concerning marriage customs more in keeping with the biblical concept of God's mercy and grace. The fact that it is quite different from the statements concerning marriage of other denominations in Liberia—or in much of Africa, for that matter—has prompted me to include the whole statement here, as it appears in the minutes.

D. ACTION OF THE CHURCH CONCERNING MARRIAGE CUSTOMS

We affirm that monogamy is God's plan for marriage, that it is the teaching of the New Testament, that it is the ideal relationship for the expression of love between man and woman, and is the proper atmosphere within which to develop a Christian family.

The entering into a polygamous marriage by a Christian, whether through the normal channels of giving a dowry, or through inheritance, or gift, is an offense against the laws of the Church.

However, we find men and women who entered into polygamous unions in ignorance of the Christian Gospel and Law, but who now express sincere faith in our Lord, manifest the power of the Spirit in their lives and desire to be baptized; yet they find themselves in certain almost unsolvable conditions, such as: divorcing the mother of a man's children, the almost impossibility of a woman's leaving her husband, or the breaking of long established families. Again, we note the New Testament treatment of certain social problems such as slavery, which were not immediately outlawed, but are manifestly unchristian, and were overthrown in time by Christianity.

In view of such, we therefore recommend:

A. Christians who enter into polygamous marriage should be excommunicated.

B. Where evidence of true faith is shown and upon approval of the District Church Council, parties to an established polygamous marriage may be baptized and confirmed. We affirm, however, that in accordance with St. Paul's teaching (I Tim. 3:2, 12) no such person, man or woman, shall be permitted to hold office in the Church or congregation or be engaged as a Christian worker. Furthermore, no such baptized person shall enter into further polygamous marriage.

C. No Christian shall be permitted to engage in the common practice of trial marriage and no candidate shall be baptized who is engaged in trial marriage. However, when the marriage negotiations have progressed to the stage of exchanging the marriage token, this marriage may be considered as a completed one and the candidate shall be led to complete the giving of the dowry as rapidly as possible.

D. In view of the fact that the families of either party often prevent the full payment of the dowry and thus prevent the completion of the marriage negotiations, if the man and woman are sincere in their desire in becoming man and wife, at the discretion of the Pastor and with the approval of the District Church Council, the union shall be recognized as valid and they may be baptized. [This is the complete action recommended by the Ministerium to the Evangelical Lutheran Church in Liberia at its Third Biennial Convention, Zorzor, Liberia, January 1951. The Church voted in favor of these recommendations. The text is taken from the Minutes of that Convention, pp. 21-22.]

Contrary to the predictions of some, the Lutheran Church was not suddenly inundated with polygamous candidates for baptism. Except for a few older men whose consciences were now unburdened so that they could accept God's grace fully, there were no immediate changes in the rate of accessions to the Church.

One most important result of the action has been that polygamy is no longer an easy excuse for the lack of church growth. The Lutherans—missionaries, pastors, and people—have been freed from the tyranny of this overrated explanation. We must now search for the real reasons for the slow growth of the Church.

If I have been a bit harsh on the missionaries, in this chapter, the reader will bear with me when he realizes that I include myself in the criticism. My own cultural overhang helped me recognize the problem. Throughout the history of the Church, it has been the missionaries who have carried the Gospel and planted churches. There are still many missionaries, and they are still instruments of God's grace. But they can move too slowly, make mistakes, and wear God's patience thin. If something I have written helps one missionary to examine himself and change his attitudes so that he becomes a more effective servant of Christ, then my effort will not have been in vain.

CHAPTER VIII

MEN AND MONEY FOR CHURCH GROWTH

DEPENDENCE ON FOREIGN MONEY

"If the Church is really to be the Church and not just a dependency of a foreign mission, it must be a responsible body, making its own decisions and, as far as lies within its powers, supporting its work with its own resources."[1] A Church that is a responsible body will be able to carry out its task of evangelism and grow rapidly. It depends on its own resources for both men and money to plant new congregations, and its plan for multiplying churches is therefore indefinitely reproducible. It does not have to wait for missionaries to be sent or funds to be appropriated before it can expand. In the preceding chapter I pointed out that there is danger that the mission will depend too exclusively on foreign missionaries to plant the Church and thereby limit the rate of expansion to the number of missionaries available. Missionaries are especially prone to put too much faith in more missionaries as the solution to the problem of slow church growth.

There is an even greater danger that the rate of church growth will be limited by the amount of foreign money available. A financially independent Church can reproduce congregations indefinitely because expansion is financed entirely from the resources of the people themselves. New congregations can be planted as rapidly as there are converts willing to support them. If, however, a pattern is established whereby each new congregation requires foreign subsidy, the expansion is directly limited by the amount of money available. The possibility for

[1] Peter Beyerhaus and Henry Lefever, *The Responsible Church and the Foreign Mission* (Grand Rapids, Mich.: Eerdmans Publishing Co., 1964), p. 10.

rapid expansion of the Church increases in direct proportion to the degree of financial independence.

This is not the same as saying that the Church will grow rapidly in proportion to the amount of money available. Too often Churches and missions under the pressure of raising money to support their programs do not distinguish between these concepts. Whether the money comes from the people or from foreign sources, they are equally happy to receive and spend it. But there is an important difference. Financial independence is a result of the faith of church members. Money raised by the village congregations themselves reflects the vitality of a Church which is able to grow. The amount available from foreign sources reflects only what some mission board or group of congregations somewhere is willing to invest, and in too many cases this figure has almost no relation to the vitality of the young Church involved. Foreign money is neither a measure of vitality nor a guarantee of church growth potential. But funds contributed by the people themselves are both.

Therefore one of the greatest services a mission can render is to teach a Church how to give. "The great mistake has been that missions have been readier to give than to train in giving."[2] Missionary culture overhang has contributed to this great mistake on three counts. (a) The missionary is likely to be so impressed by the economic weakness of the Christian community in the villages that he underestimates its ability to support an indigenous Church. (b) Western missions have established Churches along the lines of their own fixed notions about the ministry, organization, and methods of raising money, which in many cases are, in fact, beyond the ability of the people to support. To operate this Western kind of Church, it becomes necessary to depend upon foreign resources. Under such a system the successful missionary is not the one who teaches good stewardship practices to his people but rather the one who learns how to promote a project and obtain funds, from whatever source, to run it. (c) Missionaries sometimes succumb to the "western attitude of economic determinism, the belief in the

---

[2] *Ibid.*, p. 44, ascribed to Merle Davis.

determining influence of money in every sphere of life."[3] I have heard missionaries jokingly say that the trouble with their mission was that they had more money than faith. This may sometimes be too nearly the truth! Those sent out under large boards are especially vulnerable to trusting foreign money to found the Church; but missionaries of the "faith missions" are by no means immune to this attitude. When the life of the Church depends on money from abroad, the converts are not emancipated from their traditional and native spirit of dependence upon others. Instead, dependence on the chief and the society is merely transferred to the mission, which alone has the resources to operate the kind of institutional Church that has been established.[4] This becomes dollar imperialism and can be just as demeaning, in its own way, as political imperialism.

The rapid expansion of the Church among the tribes in Liberia in people-movement proportions is now possible. Tribal villagers are now ready to turn to Christ in large numbers. But rapid expansion will take place only if each new congregation is financially independent enough so that the process of multiplying churches can be reproduced indefinitely.

People-movement expansion, when correctly shepherded, enlarges both the economic and the cultural base of the Church and makes a truly indigenous, self-supported Church more feasible. This means that in the people movements about to spread through the villages in Liberia, Churches have a golden opportunity to divest themselves of dependency upon foreign funds and to adopt a new pattern of truly indigenous, self-supporting congregations. Breaking out of the old pattern will be difficult enough, and once they do break out, it will take even stronger discipline for missionaries and church leaders to resist the temptation to go back to the old system of dependence on foreign funds.

If the plan for planting churches is extravagant, it will surely be necessary to continue depending on foreign funds. Therefore it is important for the churches to learn to live within a budget,

[3] *Ibid.,* p. 41.
[4] *Ibid.*

and even more important that the budget be kept within the framework of self-support.

FORM OF MINISTRY

Mission theorists have challenged the very form of the institutional Church.[5] Not only mission theorists but theological writers in America and Europe are questioning whether the accepted Western pattern of the Church—the ministry in particular—is the best form in our modern world, especially for the younger Churches. The question then becomes, not "Who should pay the minister?" or even "How much?" but "Shall there be a paid minister at all?" After considering the difficulties of developing a ministry in Liberia supported along traditional lines, I myself almost became a convert to this view of replacing the old pattern altogether by a pattern of entirely unpaid leadership.

There are some interesting experiments using volunteer lay leaders and "tent-making" ministers now being conducted in various places in Liberia.* But these attempts are still too experimental to be recommended as the one right and effective pattern for that country. If we were starting from the beginning in a completely unoccupied field, one might recommend them. But in Liberia, hundreds of congregations throughout the country have already learned the traditional pattern of a full-time paid ministry (though paid by foreign, or in some cases government, subsidy). Surely the experimenters are to be encouraged. But rather than recommend the substitution of a completely new system, I feel that the traditional pattern of a paid ministry can be made to function on a self-supporting basis, if it is modified by a realistic effort toward self-support—especially in the event that a people-movement type of growth takes place.

At present in Liberia there are a few large, self-supporting

[5] See Roland Allen, *Missionary Methods: St. Paul's or Ours?* (London: World Dominion Press, 1956); also Stephen Neill, *The Unfinished Task* (London: Lutterworth Press, 1962), p. 61.

* Ministers who support themselves by work other than church work are often referred to as the "tent-making ministry," recalling St. Paul's occupation.

congregations. These pay a well-trained pastor, raise money through pledges and fund-raising drives, and in general function successfully in a pattern similar to that of congregations in America. In addition there are many congregations, some of them fairly large, that have a government leader or professional person of recognized prestige serving as their pastor. These do not support a full-time pastor from their offerings, but receive the benefit of a highly educated man in the pulpit. Among the tribal peoples are several hundred village congregations whose pastors are supported by foreign mission funds, "tent-making" employment, contributions from the people, or some combination of these three sources of income. These are the congregations that most concern us here, for when a people movement takes place, thousands of churches of this kind will be started.

ANALYSIS OF SELF-SUPPORT

In order to have an indefinitely reproducible pattern of church planting in these yet unevangelized tribal villages, the Churches must learn to work within a budget which can be met from contributions of the members. The question is, can the village congregation raise a budget sufficient to pay its own pastor, maintain its own buildings, and adequately support its own benevolences? Whether we can answer yes to this question depends on three variable factors in the formula for self-support. These are: (a) the number of members making regular contributions, (b) the amount of the average contribution, and (c) the size of the pastor's salary. Since the pastor's salary is by far the largest single item in the budget of the small village congregation, the first factor boils down to the number of persons contributing to the support of one pastor.

Number of Members. In the graph the number of members is represented on the horizontal co-ordinate. Note along the bottom, 50 members, 100, 200, 300. A congregation's prospects for self-support become brighter as the number of members increases. Where a village congregation has only 12-20 members, there is little chance of supporting a full-time man. Three or four congregations this size can sometimes band together and

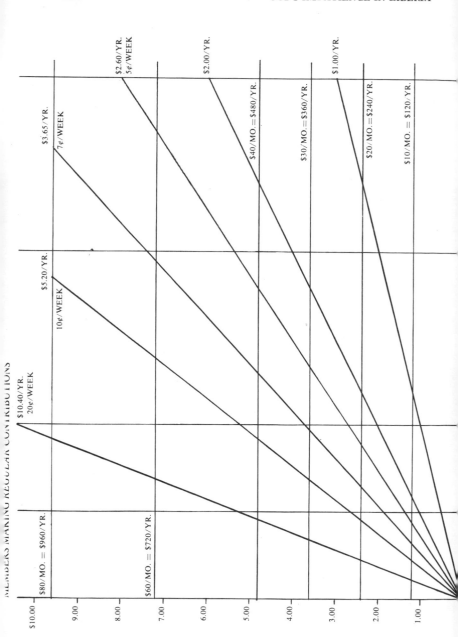

MEMBERS MAKING REGULAR CONTRIBUTIONS

$10.40/YR.
20¢/WEEK

$80/MO. = $960/YR.

$60/MO. = $720/YR.

$5.20/YR.
10¢/WEEK

$3.65/YR.
7¢/WEEK

$2.60/YR.
5¢/WEEK

$2.00/YR.

$40/MO. = $480/YR.

$30/MO. = $360/YR.

$1.00/YR.

$20/MO. = $240/YR.

$10/MO. = $120/YR.

$10.00
9.00
8.00
7.00
6.00
5.00
4.00
3.00
2.00
1.00

support one pastor, but such consolidations are generally difficult to maintain. Thus a self-supported ministry is least likely where the congregations are small, and self-support will be most difficult in sparsely populated areas. Eighty per cent of the congregations in Liberian villages have fewer than 50 members.[6] Two examples based on the most accurate statistics available will illustrate the situation.

The Protestant Episcopal Church in 1962 reported a total communing membership of 6,231. Of those, 3,076 were in seven large congregations, each with a communing membership of more than 200. The remaining 60 congregations have an average of 52 communicant members each.[7] The Methodists in 1964 reported 16,212 members, at least 4,640 of which were in 13 congregations, each with more than 200 members. The 186 remaining congregations have an average membership of 62.[8] A glance at the graph shows that for congregations of this average size to pay even the lowest-salaried evangelist, members would be expected to increase their annual contributions to an unrealistic level. When there is a people movement and a third or even half of the people in a village become Christians, the resulting large congregations are quite able to meet a budget of $30 or $40 a month. At this level an evangelist and his family can live without "making a farm" to supplement their income. Thus increases in membership are of primary importance in developing a financially independent church. The upper limit of this variable would be the number of people to whom one pastor can effectively minister. If all the members live in or near a single village, this is hardly a limiting factor at all, since self-support would be easily within the realm of possibility for a congregation in a large village.

People-movement growth will not automatically result in increases in the amount of individual contributions. It is just as possible for converts in people movements to become

[6] This figure was computed from recent statistical reports of the Lutheran, Methodist, Episcopal, and Assemblies of God Churches.

[7] Protestant Episcopal Church, *Journal, Thirty-ninth General Convocation,* p. 20.

[8] Methodist Church, "Statistics of the 114th Session . . . Liberian Annual Conference."

"wards" of the mission or missionaries as for those who come one by one.[9] But properly shepherded, the interest and vitality of such a movement can be directed toward teaching better stewardship.

Amount of Contributions. The second variable in the formula for determining the ability of a congregation to be self-supporting is the amount of the average contribution. In the graph on page 190, the diagonal lines indicate rates of giving of individual members. The steeper angles represent the higher rates of individual contributions. Examples are based on actual contributions in the Fisibu Parish (Loma) over a two-year period during which a system using numbered offering envelopes was used. The examples are fairly typical for a tribal village where there are few if any regular wage earners. For villages near industrial areas where regular employment is available, the contributions would be correspondingly higher.

To get an idea of the amount it is reasonable to expect individuals to contribute in a village congregation we may look at the following example: 7¢ a week or $3.65 a year was the minimum goal adopted by the 1959 convention of the Lutheran Church in Liberia. The average giving in all but two of the parishes has consistently fallen below this minimum goal. To a degree, the rate of giving can be increased by stewardship training and more effective methods, but it is a slow, laborious process. At this point the missionary pastor will be sorely tempted to revert to the old pattern. It is so much easier to raise a thousand dollars by writing a convincing letter to the mission board or church in America than to get five hundred average Christians to increase their annual contributions two dollars apiece.

How much can a village Christian be reasonably expected to give? A careful investigation of the village economy and the actual expenditures of an average village Christian would help us to answer this question more accurately than is possible at present. Missionaries who are not a part of the village economy nor dependent on it are likely to set the amount too low. The

[9] Pickett, *Christian Mass Movements,* p. 213.

missionary looks at the apparent poverty of the villagers and makes a comparison with the comfortable circumstances of American Christians in his home church (the effect not lessened by the guilt he feels at his own relatively high standard of living), and comes to the decision that the "poor" villagers should not have to give anything. A new missionary is more likely to think the people are desperately poor than one who has been around long enough to see a "poor man" pay $200 cash for bundles of zinc roofing or $80 for a lodge membership initiation fee. People have money for what they think is important. Money is available to support an indigenous Church. Whatever Christians formerly spent for secret society dues and initiation fees, for charms and sacrifices, or on witch doctors and diviners, is available for church support. The money that now goes to operate the *sande* and *poro* societies would be more than enough to operate an indigenous Church if, in a people movement, the Church as an institution replaced those societies. If the members come to think of each congregation as "our church," they will contribute to it as they now contribute to their ancestral cults.

Ways of Raising Money. If a missionary is likely to be surprised at the amount of money available, he will be even more surprised at the means an indigenous Church will use to collect it. Attitudes toward money and the methods of raising it vary greatly from culture to culture. The American missionary has very definite ideas about right and wrong ways to raise money, determined by his long association with American congregations where funds are gathered by methods in harmony with American culture, which bring in enough cash to keep the church going.

The Liberians' concept of how to raise money will be in harmony with Liberian culture and quite different from that of the missionaries; most American missionaries will probably disapprove of the methods used. In a Loma village the people raise money for village fines or community projects through a lump-sum head tax (one man, one dollar). This is also the way the government tax is paid ($6 a year on each house). In an economy where steady weekly income is virtually unknown, people meet their financial obligations by setting a target of a certain lump sum and working toward it. The missionary, on the other hand, is likely to feel that the head tax is inequitable and to demand that the money be raised by individual free-will donations, so that a rich man can give more than a poor man. Following his American custom he is also likely to place a heavy emphasis on weekly contributions at worship services. By this "foreign" system, the people will end up by giving two cents or five cents each. Failing to raise the money by his method, the missionary tends to discount the villagers' offering as too meager to support the programs of the congregation and learns to look for a more dependable source of funds— donations from businessmen or the wealthy—in many cases ending up by building a church with a five-thousand-dollar grant from America, in Western architectural style. The church is paid for by foreigners, looks foreign, and the villagers do not accept it as their own. Who can blame them?

Is this situation necessary? There are no holy methods for raising money; man is not justified by the means he uses to raise money for the church. The ways in which the missionary's grandfathers used to raise funds in their churches in America fifty years ago (such as pew rental) seem offensive to us now; but the methods we ourselves use will surely seem ludicrous two generations hence. Ways of raising money are strictly cultural— historical and social—phenomena. They are adiaphora, and should be left to be determined by custom or individual choice. However, depending on foreign sources, so that the pattern of church expansion ceases to be indefinitely reproducible, is more than adiaphora. This is a mistake that affects church growth and hampers the very obedience and faithfulness of the Church.

The impression that the mission has an unending supply of five-thousand-dollar grants for this and three-thousand-dollar grants for that is another factor that effectively prevents the development of a financially independent Church. Why should a poor widow give her mite when there is a missionary who knows the secret of tapping a seemingly endless supply of funds. Once the pattern of dependence has been learned, it can be changed only by conscious and determined effort on the part of all concerned. Here missionaries and Liberian churchmen are wrong to look to the boards and the folks back home for direction. For sending Churches, missions is largely a matter of raising money and training missionaries. If they keep these channels open, they are doing their part. It is up to the missionaries and church leaders on the field to use the funds and personnel supplied in such a way that the younger Church as it develops is a responsible body and not a dependency of a foreign mission.

The Pastor's Salary. Besides the number of contributors and the amount of each contribution, the third variable factor in the formula for self-support is the pastor's salary. Since this is by far the largest item in the budget of the village congregation, it will constitute nearly the whole budget, and the budget will vary according to the size of the pastor's salary.

On the graph the horizontal lines represent possible levels of a pastor's or evangelist's salary indicated as monthly rates as well as annual totals. These are the goals a congregation must reach. Look again at the graph: on the right-hand side, $10 dollars a month or $120 a year, $20 dollars a month or $240 a year, up to $80 a month, which is the approximate base salary of ordained pastors with post-high-school training—these sums represent different salary levels. The congregation must plan its budget according to the salary level of the pastor. The total giving must exceed that goal before the local church can become self-supporting.

Churches have definite concepts of what a pastor ought to be. Two of the most important criteria are: First of all, he must be one of the people, in social contact with those he serves, sharing their problems and understanding their needs. The second criterion is training. The pastor must be able to read and interpret Scripture. Most of the denominations in Liberia are rapidly raising their standards for ministerial training. The number of years of academic training is already the most important prerequisite for ordination. In many cases academic achievement is the only firm criterion.

In the Liberian village, however, these two criteria—social contact with his fellows and high rate of education—are directly contradictory. A man who can read and write will have an income ten or even twenty times higher than that of his brother who has never had a chance to go to school. After going through high school and Bible school—to say nothing of the pastors who finish college and seminary—a Liberian minister has enough years of training to command a very high salary in government or business. The missionary's concept of the ministry includes the element of sacrifice. He is likely to view the pastor as a trained man of great devotion, serving God for little material gain. This is a Western concept, developed through centuries of mendicant orders and monks who took vows of poverty, and given a fine edge by further centuries of Protestant pastors who served for less than standard wages. But the missionary himself has what seems to the Liberian a fantastically high salary, and so the Western concept is likely to be lost in transmission. Even if the Liberian pastor is willing to serve God for, say, half or a third of the salary he would receive in another field, his income is still five times as much as that of the untrained villager in his parish. This raises a class barrier between the minister and his parishioners.

The Churches in Liberia must decide where in the social structure of the villages their pastors will fit, and train men to serve the people at that level. In America and Europe a pastor has relatively high prestige in the community, but a salary no higher than that of the average member of his congregation. The training of a pastor for a Liberian village must not automatically put him on a salary scale that separates him from the members of his church. If he has too much education, for example, he may be unwilling to allow his daughter to marry the son of a villager—even the son of the chief. If his salary is so high that even the chief and traders are poor by comparison, the parishioners will be unwilling to give their money to support him.

The pay scale for evangelists and pastors in most denominations in Liberia is determined almost entirely by years of education. Not only higher pay, but ordination itself is bestowed only upon those who have reached a prescribed academic level. Thus the ordained men have an income in keeping with their years of formal training. In several denominations only ordained men are allowed to administer the sacraments or make major decisions for the congregation.

Look at the 10¢-a-week diagonal line on the graph. Even if the congregation grows to a membership of 100 and members increase their giving to an annual rate equal to what the average family pays in hut tax to the government ($5 each for a husband and wife is more than the current $6-a-year hut tax), the amount raised would still be only half what is presently paid to an ordained pastor with post-high-school training (about $1,000 a year).

No wonder many theorists feel that the only solution to the problem is to substitute a different system for the Western pattern of a paid ministry. If the present pattern means that the small village congregations are doomed for the foreseeable future to receive the sacraments irregularly because they have only the ministry of unordained evangelists, or have an ordained pastor who is socially out of contact with them and whose salary must be heavily subsidized, then truly we do need a different system, for either of these situations will prevent effective expansion of the Church. Discipling the whole nation to Christ must *not* be sacrificed on the altar of a trained, highly paid ministry.

The village congregations desperately need the services of ordained pastors who can administer the sacraments and work with the deacons and church council to make major decisions on the spot. "In the Apostolic Churches ministers and sacraments were provided for every little group of Christians; in these of our foundation they are the peculiar property of a few favored centers, while the great majority of Christians are compelled to live without any resident ministers. . . ."[10] "St. Paul certainly did not found Churches without local ministers and sacraments."[11]

We can take action to solve this problem. First, we can expect substantial increases in membership when the Church grows along people-movement lines, and pray for such in-

[10] Allen, *Spontaneous Expansion of the Church*, p. 37.
[11] *Ibid.*, p. 38.

creases. If these movements are correctly nurtured and guided, increases in rate of giving and stewardship practices will occur simultaneously with the increase in membership. But it is unrealistic to concentrate on increasing these two factors alone and expect to reach the level of self-support. If the village congregations are to support their own ordained pastors or even trained evangelists, the third factor of pastor's salary must be variable also.

THE SOLUTION MEANS SACRIFICE

It is unethical for me, a missionary, stationed on a large compound with a comfortable salary, to say that the Liberian pastor must be willing to make sacrifices. But at the risk of condemning myself, I believe this is one of the most necessary first steps for the rapid expansion of the Church. For the sake of the Gospel, "civilized," well-trained men must be willing to go back to the villages and live with their people. For these men to be in the villages and supervise the work in several congregations will not, of itself, result in a financially independent, indefinitely reproducible Church. To achieve this goal, a small town congregation of one or two hundred must be able to pay its own pastor.

Can we count on highly trained Liberian ministers, able to earn $2,000 or $3,000 a year in government, commerce, or industry, to serve tribal churches at, let us say, $500—or in the early stages of church planting, $200? Yes! Americans and Europeans have no monopoly on self-sacrifice. Heroic instances of Liberian Christian leaders renouncing the world and living a life of selfless service to the Church are well known. They are the present-day heroes (together with their wives, who often bear the burden of sacrifice) of the Gospel in Liberia.

Yet it is not realistic to count on thousands of such men to shepherd the thousands of village churches which people movements will bring into the Christian faith in the coming years, any more than it is possible to depend on thousands of missionaries for the Church to grow. These exceptional men must be supplemented by others who are a more everyday part of the newly converted tribes. To make this a reality it will be necessary for the denominations to de-emphasize educational standards for ordination and to stress spiritual qualifications for the ministry, in order to have enough pastors available for these tribal villages.

In other countries and on other continents many denominations with widely varying polity and theological positions have been able to work out a multilevel ministry. In such situations the pastors are not completely interchangeable—those with less training being limited to a ministry in the villages of the rural areas. This is what happens, in actual practice, even in the present situation in Liberia, where in theory at least unified requirements for ordination are maintained.

Five Classes of Leaders

Dr. Donald McGavran has defined five classes of leaders needed by growing Churches.[12]

1. First are the *unpaid* local leaders concerned with the inner life of the congregation. They preach and teach the Bible to the congregation and instruct catechumens. Several others may participate in this ministry—some taking responsibility to visit the sick, others calling on prospective converts. Elders and deacons or church councilmen who deal with the management of the business of the congregation fall into this category. Lay training institutes for these men are important if they are to give proper direction to their congregations.

2. Second are the *unpaid* leaders who are concerned with the propagation of the faith—men who, without pay, will go to another town to spread the Gospel. Persons in this category are willing to take full responsibility for what most paid evangelists do. They will preach in neighboring pagan villages and give literacy training and catechetical instruction. The rapid expansion of the Church depends greatly on multiplication of these first two classes of leaders.

3. Third are the *paid* preachers in small village churches, recruited largely from the adult village Christians, i.e., from

[12] McGavran, "Principles and Procedures of Church Growth," class lecture, Institute of Church Growth, Eugene, Ore., 1964.

those becoming Christians. These men do the main work of the ministry in the villages. "The day-to-day spiritual care of the sick and the suffering, help with advice and guidance in social, economic and spiritual life are all done by these preachers."[13] The salary that these men receive is within the range of realistic possibility for self-support. Their training has prepared them to preach and interpret Scripture to the members of their village congregations. When the villages become Christian, a large increase in the number of leaders at this level is necessary to shepherd the flock.

> To ordain this class of paid leaders or not is a thorny question. It is generally held that full ordination should be reserved for men with high educational qualifications. However, some Churches on New Testament grounds ordain leaders on the basis of spiritual rather than educational qualifications. In other denominations, leaders of this class carry on all the functions of the ministry except they do not administer the sacraments. Whatever a particular denomination decides to do in this regard, most of the large Churches in Asia, Africa and Latin America, depend heavily on class three leaders—men from among the village converts. These men are one with the converts in most respects and are paid at a rate comparable to the income of the average member. Thus it is possible for each village congregation to support its own pastor. These men are given as much training as the Church or mission is able to provide—naturally the more training the better.[14]

4. The fourth class of leaders includes the paid preachers who serve in large congregations in urban centers or supervise a number of village congregations in the tribal areas. In Liberia their training ranges from several years of Bible school at the eighth-grade level to high school and three years of seminary,

[13] Nirmal Minz, "Changing Image of Ministry," *National Christian Council Review,* Vol. LXXXV, No. 4 (April 1965), p. 171. Minz describes this level of ministry in the Gossner (Lutheran) Church in India, which exactly parallels the situation in many places in Liberia.

[14] Donald A. McGavran on the question of ordaining "class three" workers. From an interview, May 28, 1965.

depending on the denomination. Except in a few cases their salaries far exceed the total annual offering of the congregations they serve. This discrepancy is made up by "tent-making" employment or mission subsidy. With their level of training, many of these men could earn much more in another field. They make a sacrifice to remain in the ministry.

5. The fifth class of leaders includes those few who have completed college and seminary. They are the future bishops and seminary professors of the Liberian Churches. These are the men who will represent the Churches of Liberia in international church meetings, and decide matters of policy and plan strategy.

All five levels of leadership are important, but if the Church is to expand rapidly in people-movement proportions, the Churches must make a special effort to redefine their policy on the ministry and develop and train leadership at the first three levels. These are the leaders who can be supported by the people in an indefinitely reproducible pattern of church growth.

Where new work is started, unpaid lay leaders should guide the embryonic congregations. When these congregations recognize the value of an evangelist's services, they themselves can decide to assume his support and how much to give him. When the local congregation decides the evangelist's salary, it has a direct effect on the level of pastoral care. As the congregation grows it can afford to give more support, to a more highly trained pastor. Supervising missionaries, even Liberian pastors, are not likely to know what kind of pastoral service is being rendered by a particular village worker. The people themselves, however, will know and will contribute a salary that is more in agreement with the services rendered.

> Letting the new Christians feel their way forward to a paid ministry of class three leaders must usually be done under supervision of a missionary or well-educated Liberian pastor. Nothing is more likely to end in an unshepherded, indifferent Church than for village congregations fresh from a people movement to be left to muddle through to a responsi-

ble ministry. The indigenous theory must not mean that where a movement brings tribal groups to Christian faith, the missionary keeps hands off. The need for regular Biblical instruction, ordered worship, literacy classes, class four training, and the like, demand both regular supervision and *a leader who leads* according to a clear-cut plan.[15]

More indigenousness and more self-reliance in the Church do *not* mean less missionary planning. To have a rapid expansion of the Church by an indefinitely reproducible pattern, the missionary must consciously and deliberately turn his back on easy, quick ways of obtaining money and skilled men from foreign sources and hammer out a vigorous new plan that will result in a self-supporting village congregation.

Many missionaries who have read Roland Allen about the spontaneous expansion of the Church misunderstand their new role. "Yes," they say, "we believe in the spontaneous expansion of the Church. So, we'll run the school and the hospital and let the nationals run the Church." This is shirking the responsibility of making a bold, workable plan. *More, not less,* missionary effort and planning are involved in a people-movement expansion of the Church. Where work is already established in a mission-station pattern (missionaries supervising paid evangelists in surrounding villages), to move away from subsidy toward self-support is a difficult task. Will congregations that for years have been receiving aid to subsidize a well-trained pastor be willing to raise his salary from their own offerings? Will churches that have been content with the part-time services of a "tent-making" minister be able to find the resources to pay his full salary? They may. They are able. In parts of the world where mission funds have been cut off suddenly by war, rebellion, or intense nationalism, many younger Churches thus orphaned have not only carried on but expanded their programs. It should not be necessary to wait for disaster before the local churches in Liberia move to become financially independent and self-propagating.

[15] *Ibid.*

SELF-GOVERNMENT

The matter of financial independence is closely related to self-government. As long as the missionary or supervising Liberian pastor pays the salary of the evangelist, the latter will feel responsible to his supervisor. Even the most imaginative and resourceful evangelists will fit their ministry into the pattern of activities the missionary thinks are important. If, on the other hand, the congregation is raising the money to pay the salary, the evangelist will fit his ministry to the felt needs of the members, and this will result in a deeper pastoral concern on his part. But if the congregation pays the salary, they will expect to take a greater part in the government of the church also. When the church budget is prepared, congregation elders must be the ones who make the decisions that affect their congregation. How much they will pay and how they will raise the money, or what the duties of the evangelist will be who receives the money—all these are questions that should be decided by the congregations themselves. Even the matter of whom they call to be their pastor should be determined by the congregation.* In cases where a particular denomination's polity makes this impossible, every effort should be made to consider the needs and desires of the congregation involved before assignments are made. Where polity permits, a regional board of adjudication might be responsible for matters of discipline, so that these decisions would not be left to the supervising pastor or missionary.

Hodges says, "Perhaps we have made the mistake of thinking of self-government primarily on a national level rather than in terms of the local church."[16] To be indigenous, the Church must govern its own affairs at the village level. With an annual budget of several hundred thousand dollars a year, almost any kind of church organization can be made to function on the

---

* Churches with Episcopal polity—Methodist and Episcopalian —may have some difficulty at this point, but being aware of the problem, a bishop can take steps to compensate for it.

[16] Melvin L. Hodges, *On the Mission Field* (Chicago: Moody Press, 1953), p. 18.

national level. But where the people themselves make the decisions and pay for them out of their own offerings, there in the village the Christians will develop a polity they understand, which fits their own village situation, and for which they are financially responsible. When this happens, the Church will be no longer be a dependency of a foreign mission, but a responsible body making its own decisions and carrying on its mission, by God's help, with its own resources.

CHAPTER IX

NOW, TO FATHER A PEOPLE MOVEMENT

God is infinitely patient. His mercy endures forever when He is dealing with men's failures and weaknesses. But when it comes to telling lost men about Him and claiming them for His own, God reveals a kind of holy impatience for all men to know Him. This same holy impatience should mark His Churches in Liberia and make them ill-content with any mission methods or programs that produce little church growth or actually hinder it.

The Churches in Liberia *can* grow rapidly, especially among the hundreds of thousands of tribal villagers. Whether they will or not depends to a large extent on the leaders of the Churches, primarily the ordained ministers. It would be a mistake to expect that all ministers will take the necessary steps to achieve rapid church growth, or indeed that they even desire it. Of all the ministers in Liberia, many—especially missionaries—are not parish pastors, and so are not in a position to do much directly about the growth of the Church.

Of those parish pastors who could do something about it, some are so busy with conventional parish programs that they have no time to try new, demanding evangelistic methods. Some want the Church to grow, but are uneasy about the "people-movement" type of growth. Some are not convinced that "Gentiles" can become Christians without being "circumcised"; others fear the "circumcision party" in their particular denomination. This leaves relatively few men who are in a position to foster rapid church growth and who will dare to expect people movements to take place in Liberia.

It is to these that I address this last chapter. For you who are ready and willing to shepherd "people movements," the logistics of baptizing the 800,000 pagan villagers of Liberia—or even half that number—in the next ten years are impossible. But you must not be discouraged. Once the Church begins to grow with people-movement dynamics, the Lord of the harvest Himself will provide the needed workers. In countries around the world where such movements have taken place, leaders have been raised up from among the people being won. Liberia will be no exception.

You pastors have been trained to preach the Word and to proclaim God's promises. You know how important it is to pray for the gift of the Holy Spirit. Right proclamation and ardent prayer are basic. The church growth approach to evangelism is no gimmick that can be substituted for either. In proclaiming the Word, the importance of language study and vernacular literacy programs are self-evident. The first of these guarantees that when you interpret the Word you will be understood by those for whom you are interpreting. Literacy programs put the Word into the hands of hundreds of adults who have never had a chance to go to school, but who with ability to read their tribal language are the very ones who can bring about a people movement. If we are faithful to proclaim the Word so that it is understood, and pray fervently for the Holy Spirit—expecting something as big as a people movement to take place— God is able.

You also recognize that many methods of the past are inadequate for the rapid expansion of the Church which must now take place in Liberia. Some policies of mission boards, opinions of church leaders, and attitudes of fellow missionaries and pastors are unfavorable to the rapid expansion of the Church. But be careful. Blaming superiors or predecessors is a sterile activity. Athletes do not win races by complaining that the hurdles are too high or the track slippery. Work to make the rapid growth of the Church a possibility; consider the obstacles you meet—including outmoded methods and restrictive policies—as part of the course; but run to win.

Several specific steps must be taken. The first is often an analysis of what is actually happening in your area. This is especially important if spotty growth is already taking place. Interview the last dozen or so converts in each village. Discover whether there is some factor that binds them, or some of them, together. If they are part of a homogeneous unit of the society, you have a clue to an approachable group in that situation. This analysis is a harbinger of great growth potential.

Sometimes analysis only verifies the inadequacy of your present methods. For example, you may discover that only schoolboys or misfits are being won to the Church! Even in such cases, however, there may be a basis on which you can advance to people-movement growth. So ask yourself if there is a way that these converted schoolboys might lead their families and the rest of their tribe to full Christian commitment.

When analysis reveals two or even three patterns of accession to the Church, you have a glorious opportunity to decide which pattern is most likely to result in a people movement, and to concentrate all your energies in that direction. Along with the pattern of accession, analyze the thinking of the villagers that hinders them from becoming Christians. If there are misunderstandings as to what being a Christian means, these can be cleared away by constant repetition in teaching and preaching.

Communicate the possibilities of a people movement to Christ in your area to your lay leaders and evangelists, and through them to the pagan villagers. The importance of this can hardly be overemphasized. Lay leaders no less than missionaries and pastors must learn about the new patterns and unlearn old ones that hinder growth. Get your evangelists to discuss the difference between Christianity and the culture of Western civilization. Encourage them to let their imaginations roam freely over such questions as: What would one of our tribal villages be like if everyone became a Christian? What things would have to change? What things could remain the same? If the Philippian jailer had been a tribal villager, who-all might have been included in his household? On whom did the Holy Spirit fall? Who were baptized with him?

When you find an evangelist who understands the new possibilities of a people movement, plan an evangelism campaign for his town. Do not be in a hurry. Discover from him and from the knowledgeable lay leaders who are the important elders of the town. Identify the men who can make decisions that will affect the whole village. Then go to the chief and ask him to appoint a date when he and the village elders will be able to sit down with you and discuss the matter. Be prepared to talk to these men about becoming Christians and giving up witchcraft, sorcery, and ancestor spirit worship with the same patience and determination it would require to persuade them to break up their town and move it to a new site away from a malarial swamp. This kind of decision is not made in an afternoon. If you succeed in getting them to raise the issue of changing their religion—to discuss formally the question of whether or not to change—you will have gone a long way toward making a people movement possible.

It may be that the town as a whole will not even consider becoming Christian. See then if there is one quarter, or at least one large influential family, that will consider "following Christ together." In every instance seek to escalate the evangelistic process from the "one by one" mission-station pattern to evangelism of whole families or whole villages or even clans.

The way in which conversations with the tribesmen are carried out is important. Nothing will make Christianity seem more foreign to their whole way of life than a discussion led by a missionary according to Robert's *Rules of Order*. Talks such as I envisage should take the form of the tribal moot in the ancient sense, not the perfunctory Western business session. The evangelist and deacons will understand how to conduct such momentous "palavers." The proper form, including pronouncing of blessings, order of speakers, and exchange of gifts or whatever else is common practice, should be scrupulously observed.

When everyone has had his say and the greyest head has had a chance to express an opinion, it may be that they will have decided not to be part of a people movement into the Church. However, if favorable opinions have been expressed the evangelist and pastor will know which of the leaders may be counted upon to help sway their own families, at least. Even if the group agrees not to stand in the way of individuals or families who want to become Christians, a major victory for the Gospel will have been won. In fact, just to have had them all sit down and consider the possibility of the whole village becoming Christians together is a major step toward changing the attitude of the village.

When the whole town is discussing the possibility, the time is ripe for a potent evangelistic campaign. In parishes of the Loma district, we pull out all the stops. We use every means to bring the Gospel to their attention and urge them to make a decision about Christ. The pastor himself spends time in the village during the campaign, usually several weeks. Nurses are brought in for hygiene lectures in the various quarters. Teams of faithful laymen, especially older adults, come to the town and make house-to-house visits each day, giving a simple straight-forward witness to their faith and urging the members of each household to become Christians, or at least to come and hear the Word in the preaching services held each evening in the center of town. These services, which begin with movies or slides and include personal testimonies and preaching, come to a climax in an opportunity for listeners to be "introduced to God" (*lo Gala gaazu*). This includes confession of sins, recording of names, and assurance of God's care and His forgiveness. How patiently God has waited for the return of these wanderers—how impatiently He hastens down the road to meet them.

These converts must not be abandoned. The first two or three days after their decision are the most important in their lives. The next two or three weeks are also important. Too often converts have been told, "Come to instruction class next Thursday night." This leaves them at loose ends for days. The momentum of the decision and of the evangelism campaign is dissipated. At our Loma services converts are told to assemble without fail the next morning. All God's people—visitors, local congregation, pastor and evangelist and converts—begin the day together with worship, Bible study, Christian life instruction and prayer. After the visiting teams leave on their house-to-house rounds, the converts remain for literacy instruction.

When the first week of evening services is over, catechetical instruction classes are held every night until the class is baptized. Literacy classes and morning devotions continue every morning.

Instruction in the basic tenets of the Christian faith can be facilitated by using a series of Bible pictures. Illiterates can teach themselves and each other if they have such pictures available, either displayed on the walls in the church or, better yet, in individual take-home booklets. Someone in the class will say to his neighbor, "I know this story, but I was not in class the night they learned this story. Can you tell me what this picture is about?" Then begins Bible instruction of one illiterate by another.

Catechumens (or new converts) are encouraged to participate freely in the life of the congregation from the first. The emphasis is on aspects of Christian living—stewardship of life and possessions, doing merciful works, prayer and witnessing to others—not on a list of "Thou shalt nots."

Evangelism does not stop when many catechumens are enrolled in the class and the visiting teams and preachers go home. Regular dates are set when the pastor, evangelist, and deacons go to the homes of the converts (beginning in those which have more than one member in the class) and, in a family moot or meeting for deliberation, discuss the importance of the whole family coming to Christ together—the inadvisability of dividing the household. Villagers instinctively understand this argument. Many are glad to have it emphasized and happily join their relatives in the Church. Five families won together are of more significance than 50 individuals from different families, for if whole families are won, and the tribe learns that the pattern for becoming Christian involves whole families, then evangelism will have been escalated to the level of a people movement.

It is wise not to rush the baptism of individuals, especially young people, if there is a chance of baptizing the whole family together. If the first to confess can be encouraged to wait and talk the matter over, so that the whole family become Christians together, the wait will be well worth it.

As soon as possible the Christian congregation erects a church building. It is an error for any village congregation to continue for years worshiping in a chief's palaver hut, where they may find it impossible to meet some mornings because court is in session, or where the swearing on fetishes daily desecrates their place of worship. This is both detrimental to the growth of the church and unnecessary. There is no excuse for a congrega- tion to be for long without its own church edifice. If members and catechumens are able to build their own houses, they can build their own church building. In my own parish, several village congregations have built semipermanent church build- ings (mud and sticks, with corrugated iron roof), with seating capacities of 150-250, for less than $150 each.

Finally, when families, large groups of people, and important chiefs start to become Christian, publish the news. Where there are publications in the vernacular, see that instances of church growth get full coverage in them. English newspapers will also give good coverage, but they are less useful for spreading the concept of people-movement growth among the village "peo- ple" being won, since few read English. In Liberia, the voice of the Sudan Interior Mission, radio station ELWA, broadcasts daily in nearly a dozen vernacular languages. Establishment of new churches is news, and the announcers will gladly mention instances reported to them. There is hardly a village in all Liberia where there is not at least one radio. When villagers, gathered around the set, hear every week about large accessions to the Church in neighboring villages, or—gathered around a newspaper—read that people just like themselves, whole families, not just children who have gone to school but even the *old men*, are following the New Way, then their own resistance to the Gospel is broken down. Becoming Christians together becomes a real option to them. They begin to expect such a movement to take place in their own village. Then when the missionary, pastor, or evangelist finally comes to that village to preach the Gospel, he finds them eager, like the villagers in Ivory Coast where the Prophet Harris preached.

For generations the Churches of Liberia have been praying and hoping for the tribes of the hinterland to accept Christ. God has been patient. But now the urgent impatience in His love for lost men breaks out. The day of God's mercy has dawned. The time has come for the Churches and missions to make bold plans so that their hopes become a reality, and to work hard to carry out the plans so that they can receive in full God's answer to their prayers. God's answer is good measure, pressed down, shaken together, and running over. In the next ten years Liberian Churches can increase their membership five, eight, or even tenfold.

To that, many readers will quickly add, "God willing." I am convinced that God is willing. The question is, are we?

APPENDIX A

PERSONS INTERVIEWED

The following persons were interviewed according to the questionnaire in Appendix B. Not all the interviews are quoted or cited directly, but all of them made a contribution to my understanding of the problems and accomplishments of their respective Churches. I am grateful to each one. Their names, assignment, denomination, length of service (if known), present place of work, tribe involved (if any), and place of interview are as follows:

1. Rev. O. C. Arnes, American missionary pastor, Assemblies of God Associates. 1957-present. Greenville, African Fruit Co. In Monrovia.

2. The late Rev. J. D. K. Baker, rector, St. Thomas Episcopal Church, Monrovia. Ordained in 1926. Cape Mount as parish priest. In Monrovia.

3. Rev. Louis T. Bowers, American missionary pastor, vice president, Evangelical Lutheran Church in Liberia; pastor, Salala Community Lutheran Church. 1938-present. All parts of the Lutheran field in Kpelle tribe. At Salala.

4. Rev. Father P. Burgess, American missionary. Roman Catholic. First Secretary, Internunciature Apostolic. Monrovia. In Monrovia.

5. Mrs. Wendel L. Caldwell, widow of the late Wendel Caldwell, American missionary at Ganta (Mano) Methodist Mission. Until his death in 1965. In Eugene, Oregon.

6. Rev. John M. Carpenter, American missionary pastor, Southern Baptist Mission in Liberia. 1961-present. Sinoe (Kru). In Monrovia.

7. Rev. Burgess Carr, canon in residence, Trinity Cathedral, Episcopal, Monrovia. B.D., Cuttington, ordained 1962. In Monrovia.

8. Mr. Percy Clubine, American missionary, high-school principal, Liberian Inland Mission (formerly with Canadian Regular Baptists). 1931-64 (retired). New Cess. In Monrovia.

9. Rev. B. B. Coefield, American missionary pastor, field secretary and business manager, Methodist Mission in Liberia. 1939-present. Ganta (Mano), Monrovia. In Monrovia.

213

10. Rev. Harvey J. Currens, American missionary pastor, former president, Lutheran Mission, administrative assistant to the president, Lutheran Church in Liberia. 1927-37, 1947-present. Zorzor (Loma), Monrovia. In Monrovia.

11. Rev. David Seah Doe, pastor, First Methodist Church, Monrovia (recently moved to a ministry on the Kru coast). Cuttington. Ordained 1959. In Monrovia.

12. Rev. John B. Falconer, American missionary pastor, National Baptist Convention, U.S.A. (Formerly in Liberia as a military chaplain, U.S. Army.) Pastor, Providence Baptist Church, Monrovia; administrator, Carrie V. Dyer Hospital. 1944-present. Monrovia. In Monrovia.

13. Rev. Clifford C. Grosenbacher, American missionary pastor, St. John's Lutheran Church, Zorzor. 1955-present. Zorzor (Loma). In Zorzor.

14. Rev. H. G. Hallberg, American missionary pastor, Open Bible Standard Mission. 1962-65, leave of absence for health reasons. River Cess. In Brewerville.

15. Mrs. Daniel R. Horton, wife of Dr. Horton, pastor of St. Simon's Baptist Church, Monrovia (independent). Former missionary of the National Baptist Convention, U.S.A. (until 1929). Now a Liberian citizen. 1917-present. Bassa and Monrovia. In Monrovia.

16. Rev. Mulbah Jackson, pastor, Ebenezer Lutheran Church, Salayea. Ordained 1962. Salayea (Kpelle). In Parakwele.

17. Mr. Mulbah Jackson, evangelist for the Lutheran Church in the Gbonita Parish. Parakwele (Kpelle). In Parakwele.

18. Rev. H. H. Landrus, American missionary pastor, pilot, business manager, Assemblies of God Mission. 1935-present. Cape Palmas district 33 years, Monrovia. In Brewerville.

19. Rev. J. T. Lyons, American missionary pilot and mechanic, Mid-Liberian Baptist Mission. 1959-present. Tapeta (Mano, Gio). In Monrovia.

20. Rev. Robert G. Oberly, American missionary pastor, United Lutheran Church in America. 1925-35 (later to India). Zorzor (Loma). In Kenosha, Wisconsin.

21. Rev. Manne Paulsen, Swedish missionary pastor, Swedish Free (Pentecostal) Church. 1947-present. Voinjama, Foya Kamara (Loma and Gbande). In Zorzor.

22. Rev. S. T. Roberts, comptroller of the Government of Liberia, pastor of Patten Memorial Church (Methodist), Monrovia. Ordained 1960 after serving as a lay preacher for many years. In Monrovia.

23. Father Allen E. Smith, American missionary pastor, Order of the Holy Cross, Episcopal. 1961-present. Bolahun (Kissi). In Zorzor.

24. Miss Kay Tullis, American missionary, Liberian Inland Mission, Bible teacher in Monrovia public schools. 1940-present. Monrovia. In Monrovia.

25. Rev. Dr. T. Ebenezer Ward (retired 1958), pastor for 33 years of First Methodist Church in Monrovia and president of College of West Africa. Dr. Ward was personally acquainted with such outstanding Liberian churchmen as William Wade Harris, Bishop Samuel D. Ferguson, President Howard A. Barclay, and others.

APPENDIX B

1. Name and present position including experience.

2. How many parishioners are you responsible for in your parish?

3. What was your training when you were assigned?

4. What is the situation in your parish? Towns and preaching points?

5. How many instruction classes do you supervise? Teach?

6. What is the number in the largest class? Smallest?

7. How do you start new work in a town or village?

8. Have you started new work recently? Evangelistic? Other?

9. What is required of a candidate before baptism is administered?

10. Are there any financial requirements?

11. Do you notice any stratification in the parish as to age, sex, occupation?

12. How much does the Pastor receive? Evangelist? Where does the money come from?

13. What language is used in the service?

14. Is there a school? Is there any preference shown to Christians?

15. Is there a clinic? Who are the patients?

16. Is the population fairly stable or mobile in your area?

17. Are many whole families coming into the Church?

18. Do you have any second- or third-generation Christians?

19. What encounter do you have with Islam?

20. What growth have you noticed in the Church? What hinders/ helps growth?

21. What opportunities is the Church meeting? Missing?
22. Is there a church building?

APPENDIX C

Below is a sample of the statistical questionnaire sent to all Churches and missions in Liberia. Replies were received from: Assemblies of God; Assemblies of God, Associates; Child Evangelism; Lutheran Mission in Liberia; Methodist Church; Open Bible Standard Mission; Pentecostal Assemblies of Canada; Protestant Episcopal Church; Roman Catholic Church; Seventh Day Adventists; Sudan Interior Mission; United Pentecostal Church.

The sample shown is of the Protestant Episcopal Church of Liberia.

Study of Church Growth in Liberia

1. What is the present personnel in your mission staff in Liberia? Foreign ordained_____9_____, national ordained_____15_____, foreign lay ____27_____, national lay_____227_____.
2. What is your latest membership figure?

		BAPTIZED	COMMUNING OR FULL MEMBER
	latest figures	10,733	6,986
3. What was the member-	1962	9,043	6,159
ship in	1957	7,595	5,110
	1952	6,995	4,434
In every case the nearest	1949	6,774	3,945
year for which figures are	1939 (1938)	10,900	5,600
available.	1930	8,190	6,152
	1920	—	2,450
	1910	—	2,594
	1900	—	1,507

4. What is the source of this information?
   1. Personnel records in Overseas Department.
   2. Journal of the General Convention of the Missionary District of Liberia, April 1963.
   3. *The Episcopal Church Annual* (which was called *The Living Church Annual* through 1952, and *The American Church Almanac* through 1900). Note that no figures are available on baptized members before 1920.

BIBLIOGRAPHY

History of Liberia and Africa

Anderson, Robert Earle. *Liberia, America's African Friend*. Chapel Hill, N.C.: University of North Carolina Press, 1952.

Buell, Raymond Leslie. *Liberia: A Century of Survival, 1847-1947*. Philadelphia: University of Pennsylvania Press, 1947.

Cole, Henry B. (ed.). *The Liberian Yearbook, 1962*. Monrovia: Liberian Review Publication, 1962.

Cole, Johnetta. "Notes on Traditional Occupations and Work Patterns of Tribal Liberians." From "Northwestern University Economic Survey of Liberia"; to be published. Evanston, Ill.: Northwestern University, 1962. Staff paper, mimeographed.

Dalton, George. "The Dilemma of Piecemeal Change in Tribal Life." From "Northwestern University Economic Survey of Liberia"; to be published. Evanston, Ill.: Northwestern University, 1962. Staff paper, mimeographed.

Fage, J. D. *An Introduction to the History of West Africa*. Cambridge, Eng.: The University Press, 1962.

Gaisseau, Pierre Dominique. *Forêt Sacrée: Magie et Rites Secrets des Toma*. Paris: A. Michel, 1963.

Greene, Graham. *Journey Without Maps*. Toronto: W. Heinemann & Co., 1950.

Hailey, William Malcolm. *An African Survey*. Rev. 1956. London: Oxford University Press, 1957.

Johnston, Harry H. *Liberia*. London: Hutchinson & Co., 1906.

Junge, Werner. *African Jungle Doctor*. London: George C. Harrap & Co., 1952.

Kimble, George H. T. *Tropical Africa*, Vols. I and II. New York: Twentieth Century Fund, 1960.

Marinelli, Lawrence A. *The New Liberia*. New York: Frederick A. Praeger, 1964.

Newton, John. *The Journal of a Slave Trader (1750-1754)*, ed. Bernard Martin. London: Epworth Press, 1962.

Schwab, George, and Harley, George W. *Tribes of the Liberian Hinterland* ("Papers of the Peabody Museum of American Archaeology and Ethnology," Vol. XXXI). Cambridge, Mass.: Harvard University Press, 1947.

Wilson, Charles Morrow. *Liberia*. New York: William Sloane Associates, 1947.

Yancy, Ernest Jerome. *The Republic of Liberia*. London: George Allen & Unwin, 1959.

217

Young, James Capers. *Liberia Rediscovered*. New York: Doubleday, Doran, 1934.

Liberian Church History

Bane, Martin J. *The Catholic Story of Liberia*. New York: D. X. McMullen Co., 1950.

Cason, Walter. "The Growth of the Church in the Liberian Environment." Unpublished Ph.D. thesis, Columbia University, 1962.

Cassat, Varian H. *Liberian Palaver*. New York: National Council of Churches, 1952.

Davey, Cyril J. *The March of Methodism*. New York: Philosophical Library, 1951.

Holt, Ivan Lee. *The Methodists of the World*. New York: Methodist Board of Missions and Church Extension, 1950.

Latourette, Kenneth Scott. *A History of the Expansion of Christianity*, Vol. VII, *Advance Through the Storm*. New York: Harper & Brothers, 1945.

Liberia. Springfield, Mo.: Foreign Missions Department of the Assemblies of God, 1958.

Price, Frederick A. *Liberian Odyssey*. New York: Pageant Press, 1954.

River Cess Story, The. Des Moines, Iowa: Open Bible Standard Mission, 1963.

Southon, Arthur E. *Gold Coast Methodism*. London: Cargate Press, 1935.

Walker, F. Deaville. *The Story of the Ivory Coast*. London: Cargate Press, 1926.

Whetstone, Harold Vink. *Lutheran Mission in Liberia*. Philadelphia: Board of Foreign Missions of the United Lutheran Church in America, 1955.

Mission Theory—General

Anderson, Gerald H. *The Theology of the Christian Mission*. New York: McGraw-Hill Book Company, 1961.

Bates, M. Searl, survey committee chairman. *Survey of the Training of the Ministry in Africa*, Part II. London: International Missionary Council, 1954.

Beyerhaus, Peter, and Lefever, Henry. *The Responsible Church and the Foreign Mission*. Grand Rapids, Mich.: Eerdmans Publishing Co., 1964.

Erb, Earl S. "Bold, Creative, Long-Range Thinking," *World Encounter*, Vol. 2, No. 3 (February 1965), p. 5.

Kraemer, Hendrik. *The Christian Message in a Non-Christian World*. London: Edinburgh House Press, 1938.

Luzbetak, Louis J. *The Church and the Cultures*. Techny, Ill.: Divine Word Publications, 1963.

BIBLIOGRAPHY 219

Minz, Nirmal. "Changing Image of Ministry," *National Christian Council Review,* Vol. LXXXV, No. 4 (April 1965).

Niles, D. T. *Upon the Earth.* New York: McGraw-Hill Book Company, 1962.

Pickett, J. Waskom. *Christian Mass Movements in India.* New York: Abingdon Press, 1933.

Report of the All-Africa Seminar on the Christian Home and Family Life. Mindolo Ecumenical Center, Kitwe, Northern Rhodesia, February 17 to April 10, 1963.

Scherer, James A. *Missionary Go Home.* Englewood Cliffs, N.J.: Prentice-Hall, 1964.

Taylor, John V. *The Primal Vision.* London: SCM Press, 1940.

Trowell, H. C. *The Passing of Polygamy.* London: Oxford University Press, 1940.

*Mission Theory—Church Growth**

Allen, Roland. *Missionary Methods: St. Paul's or Ours?* London: World Dominion Press, 1956.

———. *The Spontaneous Expansion of the Church.* London: World Dominion Press, 1956.

———. *The Ministry of the Spirit.* Grand Rapids, Mich.: Eerdmans Publishing Co., 1962.

Goforth, Jonathan. *When the Spirit's Fire Swept Korea.* Grand Rapids, Mich.: Zondervan Publishing House, 1943.

**Grimley, John B., and Robinson, Gordon E. *Church Growth in Central and Southern Nigeria.* Grand Rapids, Mich.: Eerdmans Publishing Co., 1966.

**Hamilton, Keith E. *Church Growth in the High Andes.* Pasadena, Calif.: Fuller Theological Seminary, 1962.

Hodges, Melvin L. *The Indigenous Church.* Springfield, Mo.: Gospel Publishing House, 1953.

Johnson, Raymond and LuVerne. "Church Growth in the Ivory Coast." Pasadena, Calif.: Fuller Theological Seminary, 1964. Unpublished manuscript.

McGavran, Donald A. *How Churches Grow.* London: World Dominion Press, 1950; New York: Friendship Press, 1960.

**———. *Church Growth in Jamaica.* Pasadena, Calif.: Fuller Theological Seminary, 1962.

———. *Bridges of God.* London: World Dominion Press, 1955; New York: Friendship Press, 1956.

———. *Multiplying Churches in the Philippines.* Manila: United Church of Christ in the Philippines, 1958.

* See reference to "Mission Theory—Church Growth" in Introduction, p. 11.

** Indicates book belonging to Church Growth series.

**————, Huegel, John, and Taylor, Jack. *Church Growth in Mexico.* Grand Rapids, Mich.: Eerdmans Publishing Co., 1963.

———— (ed.), Guy, Hodges, and Nida. Church Growth and Christian *Mission.* New York: Harper & Row, 1965.

Nelson, Wilton M. *A History of Protestantism in Costa Rica.* Pasadena, Calif.: Fuller Theological Seminary, 1963.

Nevius, John L. *The Planting and Development of Missionary Churches.* Philadelphia: Presbyterian and Reformed Publishing Co., 1958.

Pickett, Warnshuis, Singh, and McGavran. *Church Growth and Group Conversion.* Pasadena, Calif.: Fuller Theological Seminary, 1962.

**Read, William R. *New Patterns of Church Growth in Brazil.* Grand Rapids, Mich.: Eerdmans Publishing Co., 1965.

Scanlon, A. Clark. *Church Growth Through Theological Education.* Pasadena, Calif.: Fuller Theological Seminary, 1962.

**Shearer, Roy E. *Wildfire: The Growth of the Church in Korea.* Grand Rapids, Mich.: Eerdmans Publishing Co., 1966.

**Sunda, James. *Church Growth in West New Guinea.* Pasadena, Calif.: Fuller Theological Seminary, 1963.

Vicedom, G. F. *Church and People in New Guinea* ("World Christian Books," No. 38). London: Lutterworth Press, 1961.

Church Statistics

Beach, Harlan P. (ed.). *World Missionary Atlas.* New York: Institute of Social and Religious Research, 1925.

Dennis, James S. *et al.* (eds.). *World Atlas of Christian Missions, 1911.* New York: Student Volunteer Movement for Foreign Missions, 1911.

Grubb, Kenneth G. (ed.). *World Christian Handbook.* London: World Dominion Press, issues of 1949, 1952, 1957, and 1962.

Lutheran Mission in Liberia. Biennial Conference Reports for 1930 through 1962. On file in the archives of the Lutheran Church in Liberia.

Methodist Church. "Statistics No. 1," *Minutes, Liberia Annual Conference,* January 31 to February 7, 1900.

————. "Statistics No. 1," *Minutes, Liberia Annual Conference,* March 2-7, 1910.

————. Statistical Report for 1955 Conference. Available from Methodist Board of Missions, 475 Riverside Drive, New York, N.Y. 10027 (photostat).

————. Statistical Report for 1962 Conference. Available from the Methodist Church in Liberia, Monrovia. Mimeographed.

————. "Statistics of the 114th Session of the Liberian Annual Conference," January 22-26, 1964. Mimeographed.

————. Division of World Missions. Reports to the annual meetings of the Board of Missions: 22nd, 23rd, and 24th, for 1962, 1963, 1964, respectively.

Parker, Joseph I. (ed.). *Interpretive Statistical Survey of the World Missions of the Christian Church.* New York: International Missionary Council, 1938.

Protestant Episcopal Church. *Journal, Thirty-seventh General Convocation,* Robertsport, Liberia, April 27 to May 1, 1960.

————. *Journal, Thirty-ninth General Convocation,* Kakata, Liberia, May 2-6, 1962.

Anthropology

Barnett, H. G. *Innovation: The Basis of Culture Change.* New York: McGraw-Hill Book Company, 1953.

Firth, Raymond (ed.). *Man and Culture.* London: Routledge & Kegan Paul, 1957.

Hoebel, E. Anderson. *Man in the Primitive World.* New York: McGraw-Hill Book Company, 1958.

Hunter, Guy. *The New Societies of Tropical Africa.* London: Oxford University Press, 1962.

Kiesing, Felix M. *Cultural Anthropology.* New York: Holt, Rinehart and Winston, 1958.

Kroeber, A. L. *Anthropology, Race, Language, Culture, Psychology, and Pre-History.* New York: Harcourt, Brace & Co., 1958.

Malinowski, Bronislaw. *Dynamics of Culture Change.* New Haven: Yale University Press, 1945.

————. *Magic, Science and Religion.* Garden City, N.Y.: Doubleday-Anchor Books, 1948.

Murdock, George Peter. *Africa.* New York: McGraw-Hill Book Company, 1959.

Nida, Eugene A. *Customs and Cultures.* New York: Harper & Brothers, 1954.

Winick, Charles. *Dictionary of Anthropology.* Paterson, N. J.: Littlefield, Adams & Co., 1961.

Other

Lock, Walter. *The Pastoral Epistles* ("The International Critical Commentary" series). New York: Charles Scribner's Sons, 1924.

Luther, Martin. "Of Church Rites," *Book of Concord.* St. Louis, Mo.: Concordia Publishing House, 1957.

————. "To Philipp Melanchthon, Wartburg, August 1, 1521," *Luther's Works,* Vol. 48, *Letters I.* Philadelphia: Fortress Press, 1963.

INDEX OF SUBJECTS

223